Matthias Vercauteren

Football Management

Football Management

Sue Bridgewater
Warwick Business School, University of Warwick, UK

© Sue Bridgewater 2010

All rights reserved. No reproduction, copy or transmission of this
publication may be made without written permission.

No portion of this publication may be reproduced, copied or transmitted
save with written permission or in accordance with the provisions of the
Copyright, Designs and Patents Act 1988, or under the terms of any licence
permitting limited copying issued by the Copyright Licensing Agency,
Saffron House, 6–10 Kirby Street, London EC1N 8TS.

Any person who does any unauthorized act in relation to this publication
may be liable to criminal prosecution and civil claims for damages.

The author has asserted her right to be identified as the author of this work
in accordance with the Copyright, Designs and Patents Act 1988.

First published 2010 by
PALGRAVE MACMILLAN

Palgrave Macmillan in the UK is an imprint of Macmillan Publishers Limited,
registered in England, company number 785998, of Houndmills, Basingstoke,
Hampshire RG21 6XS.

Palgrave Macmillan in the US is a division of St Martin's Press LLC,
175 Fifth Avenue, New York, NY 10010.

Palgrave Macmillan is the global academic imprint of the above companies
and has companies and representatives throughout the world.

Palgrave® and Macmillan® are registered trademarks in the United States,
the United Kingdom, Europe and other countries.

ISBN 978–0–230–23841–1   hardback

This book is printed on paper suitable for recycling and made from fully
managed and sustained forest sources. Logging, pulping and manufacturing
processes are expected to conform to the environmental regulations of the
country of origin.

A catalogue record for this book is available from the British Library.

A catalog record for this book is available from the Library of Congress.

10 9 8 7 6 5 4 3 2 1
19 18 17 16 15 14 13 12 11 10

Printed and bound in Great Britain by
CPI Antony Rowe, Chippenham and Eastbourne

To my sons, James and Sam

Contents

List of Figures

LIST OF TABLES

The writing of this book on football management is intended to work on two levels. First the book aims to identify lessons which business managers can learn from reflecting upon the challenges of working in this turbulent, results-driven sector where football managers try to get teams of highly talented individuals to perform week in, week out. Second, this is a book about and for football and football managers. Having been privileged to work with football managers, football bodies and football clubs for almost ten years, the impact of shortening tenure, the massive rate of churn of football managers and the pressures under which they work are clear to see. It is hoped that this book might offer useful insights for managers, prospective managers and those who employ them.

At first glance, the topic of the book may appear to be narrow – why football management in England? Why not focus also on football management in other countries? The reasons are two-fold. The systems in football clubs vary country by country, so that models such as Sporting Director and head coach predominate in many countries. As the challenges of this system are somewhat different and it would be so difficult to capture all of this in one book, I decided to focus on exploring football management in one context. Second, English football, particularly the Premier League, attracts a global audience. Accordingly management of these clubs involves management of multi-cultural teams of players, international media and indeed involves many international managers – Roberto Mancini, Avram Grant, Roberto Di Matteo, Rafa Benitez and Paolo Sousa being just some of the managers currently managing in the English game. The book may centre on management in the English leagues, but these are of global interest.

In writing this book I have drawn on the insights which I have gained since becoming involved in football in 2001. I owe my involvement in the game to many people and, whilst it is hard to single out individuals for thanks among so many who have helped to spark my interest and enhance my understanding of football management, I could not let this opportunity pass without extending particular thanks to John Barnwell and Howard Wilkinson at the League Managers Association, for originally championing qualifications for football managers and choosing Warwick Business School to work with them on the Certificate. My thanks also to Richard Bevan, Graham Mackrell, Frank Clark, John Duncan, Olaf Dixon for their ongoing support and commitment and to everyone at the League Managers Association for being a joy to work with. Thanks also to the Professional Footballers Association, to Gordon Taylor, Pat Lally and Jim Hicks for their generous support for the Certificate in Applied Management for football managers and to everyone at the Football Association, particularly Danielle Every and John Peacock, for their help and support over the years. Many thanks to Deloitte and Touche Sport for providing me with access to their excellent reports on football finance. These are truly invaluable to anyone who wishes to understand the challenges of football management.

The analysis and discussion in this book are based on interviews with a number of football managers who kindly gave their time, as well as on research into football management which I have conducted over the years. Any errors or omissions are down to the author alone. The interviewees are intentionally not named in the text – I would prefer to highlight the issues rather than the individual or club concerned – but they know who they are and my thanks go to them and indeed to all the football managers and prospective football managers with whom I have had the pleasure to work. May you all reap the successes you richly deserve for the time and commitment which you have shown to preparing yourself for a challenging profession.

SUE BRIDGEWATER
Warwick Business School

The Football Management Context

Mid January 2010 sees the familiar trend of football managers parting company with their clubs repeating itself. So far this season, twenty three managers have been dismissed and six have resigned (Mark Robins: Rotherham to Barnsley, Paul Lambert: Colchester to Wycombe, Gary Waddock: Aldershot to Wycombe, Hans Backe from Notts Co., Owen Coyle, Burnley to Bolton and Paul Hart from QPR. The predictable cull of football managers, often after brief periods in charge of their respective clubs, is sometimes greeted with sadness but often with relief and – even – joy by fans. Football's "sack race" seems to have become as much of a spectacle as the matches the manager presides over. At a recent Ipswich Town match, the Sky summarizer commented that more cameras were focused on Roy Keane's reactions from the dugout than on the match action.

Football management is an industry so turbulent that it must surely be without parallel. Whilst CEOs, Creative Directors, Head Masters, might be judged on results, often in the short-term, maybe with high levels of public scrutiny, few face the extremes of football management. This season, John Barnes was given eleven games in charge of Tranmere Rovers, in 2007–08 Martin Allen went after four games in charge of Leicester City, Dave Watson after losing a pre-season friendly at Tranmere in 2002–03, Steve Claridge from Millwall before a game had been played of the 2005–06 season and Leroy Rosenior after some ten minutes as manager of Torquay, before a change of ownership took the club in a different direction.

The average tenure of football managers is now just under a year and a half and declining. Indeed the four managers dismissed from the Premier League in 2008–09 (Ince, Adams, Scolari and Ramos) lasted an average of around six months. Table I.1 shows the departures in each league during the 2008–09 season.[1]

Table I.1 Departures by league 2008–09

League	Dismissals	Resignations	Total
Premier League	4	7[2,3,4]	11
Championship	8	2	10
League 1	14	1	15[5]
League 2	7	2	9
Total	33	12	45

Later in this book, data on football management are studied to explore various different phenomena. These are studied from the beginning of the 1992–93 season, when the Premier League was formed. Only one manager, Sir Alex Ferguson, has been in charge for this whole period. Up until the end of the 2008–09 season he had seen 751 football managers come and go (642 of these were dismissed, 109 managers resigned, 62 of these to progress on to other clubs). Together with the other 91 incumbents – and not to mention numerous caretakers and other temporary managers – and the 29 changes so far this season (2009/10), that makes 871 football managers other than him employed in just over 17 years: almost 50 managers per season. In other words, every season more than half of all 92 football clubs change their managers. Table I.2 shows the changes in football manager tenure since 1992.

From the outside, changing football manager to shake things up, to bring in a new face, might seem part of the interest of the game. Endless discussion of the merits of appointing an up and coming star as new manager versus a time-served manager, of the style of football played, of whether one manager is more success-ful than another are entertaining to those whose livelihoods do not depend on the outcome. And outside of the highest levels of football management, livelihoods do, as average salaries are far lower than most people guess, job security minimal and the levels of pressure such, that one wonders why anyone would do it – other than that these are people whose entire working lives have been spent in football and who have a passion for football that keeps them coming back for more.

Yet the consequences of this level of turbulence are hard to contemplate. What would happen to our schools, businesses,

Table I.2 Football manager tenure 1992 to date

Season	Tenure (years)	% change
1992–93	3.12	n.a.
1993–94	2.3	−26.3
1994–95	2.55	+10.9
1995–96	2.33	−8.6
1996-97	2.42	+3.9
1997–98	1.81	−25.2
1998–99	1.68	−8.2
1999–00	2.04	+21.4
2000–01	2.13	+4.4
2001–02	2.04	−4.2
2002–03	2.02	−1
2003-04	2.08	+3
2004–05	2.23	+7.2
2005–06	1.84	−17.5
2006–07	1.89	+2.7
2007–08	1.53	−19.05
2008–09	1.47	−3.9

hospitals if half of them changed leader every year? What kind of market does that create for labor? What kind of cost does it place on these organizations to pay off previous leaders, hire and support the new incumbent? What are the implications for the culture of the organization? For the people who are being led, "my way or the highway" takes on a whole new meaning when there are a a veritable spaghetti junction of different roads that this array of managers may favor. Not that way, this way! That was half a season and two managers ago.

Over time, football has gone through a period of radical change, of rapid commercial development and growth. Alongside the increasing broadcast revenue and ability to attract the best players into the English game, there have been negative episodes such as the demise of ITV Digital and Setanta and highly publicized financial problems at some clubs as player wages have increased, sometimes to levels above the total revenue of the club.

Football management is now a profession acted out under the spotlight, judged – often harshly – in the short-term based on highly public performances by a set of talented individuals who often earn more than their managers and whom the football manager must motivate to deliver week in week out.

This book attempts to offer insights into football management based on:

- Data on various aspects of football manager performance from 1992 to date.
- Interview data with football managers.
- Learning from management theory.

Using these different sources, the book will try to present a comprehensive picture of the challenges and also explore how these challenges shed light on issues which also apply to managers in a broader range of results-driven, talent management situations.

Through the goldfish bowl

It is hard to imagine just what it would be like to be a football manager unless you have dealt with the unique combination of managing in the spotlight, under intense pressure and with the lack of control over outcome so that, once the players cross the line, no matter how much you gesticulate on the touchline, you have limited ability to influence the course of the game.

Whatever you have practised in training, whatever game plan you might have prepared might be useless after the first kick of the game – a goal conceded, a penalty given away, a player sent off. Football management is management in an exceptionally unpredictable world. One of the main reasons that fans remain in thrall to the game of football is that, unlike going to the theatre or watching a film, we never know what the end will be. That is great for spectators, less good for fans whose hearts are in their mouths with every kick and worse still for the football manager whose job and livelihood may rest on the outcome.

"You are never more than six games away from getting the sack", or so popular myth would have it.

Whilst some football managers progress their way up the ranks from coach to assistant manager to manager and pick up hints and techniques from managers they played under and those whom they work alongside, others are thrust straight into the spotlight. As Table I.2 shows, football managers have an average life span of just under one and a half years in the role and almost half of all first-time managers never get a second chance to manage.

In 2008–09, the higher up the leagues you managed, it seemed that the greater the pressure and the less the patience of Boards of Directors. Last season, in the English Premier League, the four sacked managers, Ince, Scolari, Adams and Ramos, had an average tenure of less than six months. This was at odds with the trends of the last few seasons in which Premier League tenure had been longer and there were fewer dismissals, as you might expect, given the more experienced and successful managers who hold these top positions. It is certainly a challenge for young managers, no matter how great they were as players, to come in at that level and succeed.

There is little room to make mistakes, football management is management in the full glare of the media spotlight, managing in a "goldfish bowl" where every action and gesture is on view. Most senior managers can recall one or two episodes along the way where things didn't go to plan, for which they took the consequences, minimized the damage, learnt a valuable lesson and moved on to become better managers. No such chance for many football managers. From the first match, fans, media, Board and players are watching. Every decision will be analyzed, every gesture replayed on television and discussed in the media, on football phone-ins and on internet web-boards. This is an exceptionally steep learning curve and there is no chance of making mistakes and learning from them without anyone noticing.

It is almost comical to talk to managers the day after a match – not just after a "big" match but any match – and to realize how many of them have lost their voices, have screamed themselves hoarse from the touchline, in the heat of the action. Comical, except when allied to the information on stress management and the number of heart problems among football managers who cope with these pressures once or twice a week over an extended period.

As a football fan – a Sunderland fan – I have been part of the crowd on occasions when frustrated fans have leveled abuse at players, manager and even Board of Directors. Most commonly, when a run of results goes against the team, the manager takes the flack, irrespective of whether the collective failings of the team are down to a lack of finance, not having players of sufficient quality or individual player mistakes.

I have been privileged to have the opportunity to work with young coaches, prospective and current football managers on the Professional Footballers Association and the League Managers' Association's Certificate in Applied Management at Warwick Business School, the University of Warwick. The development of this course provided initial opportunities to research the world and challenges of football management, which have been added to over the years by ongoing analysis of football manager trends for the LMA, research conducted on behalf of the Football Association and presented to various football bodies and clubs.

Given my ongoing involvement in football management, it has always been my concern that this book work on a number of levels:

- About football management and providing insights, which might be of interest to football managers and football bodies.
- Drawing on relevant management theory to put into broader context some of the phenomena in football management.
- Adding to the body of existing football management research by providing new analysis of quantitative and qualitative data.
- Of broader interest to other managers who face situations which are similar to those facing football managers.

This combination is already one which has brought about many sleepless nights. Overriding all other concerns, however, is that the data are used responsibly. It is essential that I do not compromise any of those who have responded to my panic-ridden requests for additional insights into various aspects of football management and have given of their time and opinions to make sure that I can see into their world with as much accuracy as is possible for an outsider, a non-football person.

The more I speak to football managers, the more I realize that no one who has not been there with that combination of different pressures will ever know what it is like to be a football manager. But if football management is life in the goldfish bowl, I am – rather like Alice and the Looking Glass – privileged to have been offered a unique view "through the goldfish" bowl. For that reason, the only data attributed to particular managers are those which have already been published in the public domain. All other data are treated – as is common with much academic research – anonymously. They are used to gain insights into the issues rather than to be identifiable to particular managers. My thanks go out to all the football managers who have helped – they know who they are. Thanks also to the PFA and LMA for the chance to work with coaches and managers and particularly to John Barnwell, whose idea it was to provide more training in management for football managers, and whose enthusiasm for the project has never dimmed.

Book structure

The chapters in this book look in greater detail at various aspects of football management and what it offers us in broader understanding of the issues facing management.

The book begins with a discussion of why we might use sport in general, and football in particular, as a vehicle to understand other areas of management.

Chapter 2 explores the world of the football manager. It begins with a discussion of the theory on leadership and the different ways in which the role of the leader in an organization might be understood. It then uses this understanding to explore the context, the task and the characteristics and abilities of successful football managers.

Chapter 3 discusses the nature of success in football management and looks at different ways in which this might be understood and measured. It then debates the influence of various factors – such as finance, management experience and the playing experience of the individual to see what impact these have both on success and whether someone is perceived to be successful. The chapter concludes with a brief discussion of findings from research into football managers and success carried out by Bridgewater, Kahn and Goodall (2010 forthcoming).

Chapter 4 looks at the issues of succession. Does changing the football manager improve performance, make no difference or indeed worsen performance of the club? If – as seems to be the case – changing the manager is of little long-term benefit to the club, why does this happen?

Chapter 5 explores further the turbulent world of football management, looking at the ups and downs which characterize football management careers and the impact which these may have on individuals at different stages in their careers.

Finally, Chapter 6 draws together some of the findings from previous chapters and discusses these in relation to the broader field of management, to see what we can learn from football management.

CHAPTER 1

What Can Business Learn from Football and What Can Football Learn from Business?

At its inaugural League Managers' Association Management Conference, successful football managers including Iain Dowie and Stuart Pearce identified a range of lessons which sport can learn from business – such as long-term strategic planning, goal setting and the value of personal development. Conversely, there are also valuable lessons which business can learn from sport. Among these Iain Dowie includes the fact that sports stars and managers learn how to operate in pressurized situations, have excellent understanding of how teams work and they work in the ultimate results business (Bill Wilson, "Boardroom lessons for the dugout", BBC Website: http://news.bbc.co.uk/1/hi/business/8278449).

Such are the parallels between sport and business, and in particularly football and business, that Bolchover and Brady (2002) maintain in their book *Business Lessons from the Dugout* that: "Had football been an American sport, it would have been the dominant business model of business management years ago."

When presented with data on the turbulent nature of the football management profession and the challenges facing football managers in achieving success, managers from many sectors respond to and identify with the challenges of a football manager as an analogy for their own challenges. These challenges include:

- *Tenure is becoming ever shorter.* Being a football manager – rather than first team coach or Head of Academy brings a higher profile, possibly higher rewards but it is, as one football manager put it: "like a game of snakes and ladders.

One moment you are cock of the walk, riding high and everyone wants to know you. Then you are sacked and after a few days the phone stops ringing." Shortening of tenure and the trade off between high rewards and high pressure are common to several different types of leader – CEOs, Headmasters, Deans – not just to football managers.

- *Football is a results business.* Popular press would have it that you are never more than six games away from the sack, no matter how good your previous record has been. Performance in football is clear, measurable and the results – league tables, reports, ranking of players and manager are extremely public. This ranking and the use of league tables is now increasingly widespread in sectors as broad ranging as education, consumer businesses, financial institutions and commerce.
- *Football managers must get the best out of talented individuals and prepare them to work effectively as a team.* Talent management is a challenge facing many managers of knowledge workers, creatives, specialists. Indeed any sector in which there is a scarcity of available talent and the organization must reach, attract and retain this talent in the face of competition.
- *Dealing with "Match Day."* Once the players cross the line onto the pitch, the football manager has limited ability to change the outcome of the match but is held accountable for the performance.

Managers tell us that they are increasingly judged on results – in education, for example, league tables are used to ranks schools and Universities, to make judgments on quality, and in industry, profits announcements can trigger sharp rises and falls in share prices.

The position of "leader" can often be lonely. It is increasingly likely that the Chief Executive, Head Master or Dean may pay the price for poor performance of the whole organization. The tenure of a Chief Executive may not be quite as short as that of a football manager, but has certainly declined markedly over the last decade.

Knowledge workers, academics, performers in the arts, lawyers, accountants – the pool of talented individuals who form the lifeblood of many organizations are increasingly mobile, individualistic and may move between organizations to rise up the ranks rapidly.

"Talent Wars" which mean that leaders need to attract, retain and sometimes decide to let go of the key individuals who make up their teams show many of the characteristics of the football team full of stars and the leader's challenge to manage these individuals may also be complex and challenging.

Being successful as a leader in any of these sectors requires, as Dowie says, the ability to take difficult decisions, remain calm and cope with life in the spotlight whilst building teams who deliver winning performances consistently.

Harry Redknapp, reflecting on the football manager's task, said in the *Daily Mail* (14 January 2007) that the most important things for a football manager were good players and knowing how to get the best out of them. This book begins which a discussion about the key challenges for a football manager and a reflection on what it takes to be successful as a football manager. It then goes on to consider some of the other management questions for which football management can provide insights, such as the impact of turbulence and managerial changes and what we can learn from football management that will help other types of business leader.

This chapter begins with a brief summary of the characteristics of the football manager's world.

What characterizes football management?

It is 24/7

During the football season, games come thick and fast. Particularly in the English Football leagues, a team may have two matches a week. Before and after matches the manager will have media commitments – he may be expected to hold a press conference before the match to discuss how the team will play. Depending on the level at which he manages, this might be with local press or else to a full press room full of national press, television and radio.

There is not always sufficient money for teams to stay in a hotel the night before a match, and only exceptionally outside the top tier is there money to fly longer distances. So the manager, coaches and team are locked into a relentless cycle of training,

travelling and playing matches. A poor result is compounded by
the knowledge that the return journey will take hours and – after
an evening match – may mean players and manager returning
home in the middle of the night.

Resources may be scarce

Generally, football managers are under pressure to push on to the
"next level," whatever that level may be. So, whilst a Championship
(second level) club may seem to have untold riches to a lower
league club, the range of resources may vary considerably between
teams who have just been relegated from the Premier League
(highest league) and still have parachute payments (an extra payment designed to soften the blow of going down a level and help to
prevent the financial difficulties which faced clubs who had over-
extended to make the step up) and those who have over-achieved
even to be in the league. Similarly there are three or four groups of
clubs within the Premier League who may be almost mini-leagues
or groups within the larger group.

Competition – and moving up to the required level – may be
tough given the respective level of available resources:

> When we went up into the Championship we did really well
> for the first part of the season, but given our squad size, once
> we began to get injuries and suspensions we just did not have
> the strength in depth to compete.

Football managers often discuss having to move players up
early from lower levels (reserves or second string or perhaps
from youth levels) before they are ready to cover resource
gaps.

Resources may need to be used flexibly

Bolchover and Brady (2002) reflect on Drucker's (1988) *Harvard
Business Review* metaphor of an orchestra to describe the 'new

organization.' This 'orchestra,' he argued, was full of high-level specialists under the leadership of a charismatic conductor. Bolchover and Brady argue for football management as a more useful metaphor for the challenges of many organizations because:

> the pool of talent from which to select orchestra members is, if not inexhaustible, certainly relatively deep. (Bolchover and Brady 2002: 9)

Where resources are limited, however, as in the previous example of a team making the step up to compete at a higher level among rivals with higher levels of resources, football managers may need to deploy their resources flexibly. The concept of using someone as "cover" or playing them out of position is fairly common. He played on the left (although he is usually more comfortable playing in the middle) and so on.

Indeed, the term 'utility player' has been coined to describe a player who – whilst he or she has a specialism – can equally be used effectively in a variety of roles. One such player, is the current England international, James Milner, who England Manager Fabio Capello has used in a variety of different roles ("James Milner hoping versatility can help aid his world cup cause," Alan Dawson, *Wolverhampton Express and Star,* 15 October 2009).

It is this need for flexible use of resources which prompts Bolchover and Brady to argue that football is a better metaphor for today's organizations than an orchestra – in which you could hardly say "I know you play trombone but could you just step in as first violin for the day?"And this flexibility can be vital for the success of football clubs. Sometimes resources are constrained, so managers may need players who can play in a range of different positions to cover for injuries and suspensions.

As in football clubs, the current climate means that many organizations are facing lean times. It may not be at the manager's behest to bring in additional resources and so success must be achieved by making best use of the resources that already exist within the organization.

The ultimate results business

Football has clear measures of performance: three points for a win and one for a draw, goal difference, goals for and against, win ratios and statistics for all aspects of on-the-pitch performance, which are captured in minute detail by television coverage and specialist analysts. These are scrutinized by fans, media and other stakeholders and any dip in form results in speculation over the manager's job security. Promotion from the English second tier into the Premier League is worth an estimated £60 million. For the two teams which contest the third promotion place, this prize rests on a single match: ninety minutes – the single "richest" sporting contest in the world. Even league position in the top division in England determines the share of broadcast revenue gained by each club. Points really do mean prizes!

As Chapter 3 will go on to discuss, however, football manager performance is not as simple as this may imply. Sometimes fans and media will be unrealistic in their expectations of what is possible. Over-achieve and gain promotion, start the next season well and the fans may expect a football manager to qualify for Europe (the highest level of achievement possible in the English football league structure). If the manager is unable – as might be anticipated – to deliver this level of performance over a sustained time period, he may pay the price with his job, no matter how unrealistic the expectations of those making the decisions.

Short time horizons

Eleven matches – less than ten weeks in charge; four games – gone three weeks into the season. These timescales, or less, may face football managers. Whilst many businesses have short, and shortening, time horizons, few have quite such short periods in which to deliver performances and build teams. Extreme – and ridiculous – though it may be to expect someone to deliver in this timescale, we can learn from football managers both what might be needed to hit the ground running, to deliver results quickly and what happens if organizations judge results too quickly and change managers in pursuit of short-term gains.

Managing today's players

It is increasingly difficult for the manager to motivate, reward and sanction the star players of the twenty-first century because they are paid more than their managers and have an increasing ability to walk away when they want. Current examples might include Cristiano Ronaldo's move to Real Madrid and Joleon Lescott to Manchester City.

If a manager sanctions the player for not behaving in an appropriate way, the player can choose to walk away rather than to accept the sanction. Contracts are no real deterrent to a player moving and there have been instances of players forcing the hand of manager and club by refusing to play, or by expressing dissatisfaction and a wish to move in the media. Put simply, the power lies more with these talented individuals than it does with the manager.

Top football players have a limited playing career and are entitled to maximize their earnings and success while they have the chance. Yet many are seen as increasingly fickle individuals who will move for the highest pay cheque rather than remain loyal to the club who gave them a chance or their local club, as used to be the way. Football managers also face difficulties in attracting the best players. Players can pick and choose between deals and may be swayed by the club's location, which other big name players are playing there, the likelihood of winning silverware or competing in Europe. The challenges of these "talent wars" also change the dynamics of the football manager's role. Several managers refer to the need to "sell" their club to prospective new players. Whilst ten years ago it would have been unusual for a football manager to begin pre-season training without a full squad in place, now clubs – who are not first choice for players – will still be signing players up until and beyond the start of the season. The task of building team unity and deciding the best formation may not begin until into the new season and the first managerial casualty – Bryan Gunn at Norwich City – came after two matches, only one of those a league match. At this point the manager may not have a settled team or even know who his final squad will be.

Talent wars are not restricted to football. The parallels between the challenges facing a football manager and other managers in the knowledge economy emerge more fully in the discussion of the football manager's role in Chapter 2 (see page 31).

Knitting together specialists

Success for a football manager, as for managers in many other sectors, does not only depend upon his own performance but upon getting the best out of others. In this case the "others" are a team of highly paid, talented individuals with different specialisms.

As in many cases, the football manager has to knit together a team of specialists, in his case goalkeeper, defence, midfield and strikers. Success depends on all of these delivering on the day. If the strikers can score goals but the defence concede more, the goalkeeper lets down the defence by making blunders or is repeatedly left exposed by the defence, then the team will not succeed. All parts of the team must work together for the whole to succeed.

Not only must the specialists be knitted together, but the specialists comprise a set of talented individuals, and talented individuals – artists rather than soldiers – are not always the easiest characters to work with. Gilmore (2001) refers to the difficulties of working with "mercurial" characters.

Delivering on match day

Many sectors have a "match day," the need to deliver a good performance on a sales pitch, in a difficult customer situation, in a key interview or presentation. For many sectors this is their "match day."

Whatever has been practiced, whatever skills have been trained into staff, no matter how much team building activity has taken place and experience the staff have, occasions will present themselves when individuals and teams need to put into effect the performances expected of them by their leaders.

It may be that the leader is not there to oversee every performance – or may be there and unable to influence the outcome once the particular performance is underway. This is what the football manager goes through on the touch line. Research points to the stresses placed on managers once their players have stepped over the white line onto the pitch. Any amount of shouted instructions and gesticulation from the touchline has limited effect. Yes, tactical substitutions are possible up to a point, but these will make little difference if the team is 3–0 down early in the match and headed for a heavy defeat. The leader might be able to motivate and get things back on track with a team talk but, other than this, can only watch and consider how he or she might better prepare the team for the next such occasion.

In the spotlight

Football manager performance is carried out in the spotlight. Virtually every move, every decision must be made in the knowledge that others will revisit this, analyze it from different angles and offer opinions on whether or not this was the correct thing to do.

Few managers are given quite such a level of attention, even those in high profile roles, which attract significant media attention and have large meetings or public gatherings. Where roles are high profile, they tend to be given to managers who have worked their way up through the system and have experience of dealing effectively with these situations.

A football player may have become accustomed to significant media attention, but may be unprepared for the types of situations and questions which come with the new role. This is learning without the ability to make and learn from any mistakes.

Under pressure

As a result of all of the above, football management is an incredibly – perhaps uniquely – pressurized role. The combination of scrutiny, short horizons, lack of control over talented, perhaps unpredictable, individuals is one which places considerable pressure on them.

These pressures, visible in growing bags under the eyes and highly publicized health conditions, serve as a cautionary tale for managers in all sectors to appreciate the toll that living with this kind of pressure can have on health, relationships and family life.

How does that help us to learn about management?

The next four chapters look at different aspects of football management. These are each discussed in relation to the relevant debates in management literature to see what insights can be gained. In each case, data are drawn from football manager statistics or interviews to explore the issue.

Some of these will get into realms which might seem confusing to the non-football specialist, although most fans will be easily able to understand the debates. For clarity, however, a glossary of football terms is presented at the end of the book and might be useful as a reference alongside these chapters. Each chapter contains a discussion of the broader implications of what the chapter reveals.

CHAPTER 2

Life in the Fast Lane

Introduction

This chapter discusses the challenges of being a leader, or manager, in football. Analysis of these challenges is based on interviews with football managers as well as on data drawn from media interviews with football managers. The challenges are mainly discussed using the football managers' own description of what they do and what they consider to be the main issues.

Before debating the specifics of the football manager's role, the chapter begins with a brief summary of leadership literature in management theory, to provide insights into how leadership has been understood and studied over time.

This theoretical review is important because different schools of leadership thought argue that the individual leader has greater or lesser importance. Alongside those who believe that individual characteristics or behavior are the greatest determinants of success, are those who argue that factors in the organizational context – such as resources, organizational structure, clear roles and responsibilities – play as great, if not a greater, role in influencing the leader's success. The review of football managers as leaders then goes onto describe both the individual and context aspects of their role.

Leadership theory

To be a leader, you need followers

Management research suggests that leaders have "a possibly crucial impact on the performance of the organizations they head" (Berkeley Thomas 1988). As Goodall, Kahn and Oswald (2008) put it: "Leaders matter. Little is known, however, about why some leaders are successful while others are not." In fact, the evidence about whether or not leaders have a major effect on performance is divided. Theory divides into the "individualistic" strand, which argues that leaders can affect the performance of organizations, and the "contextual school" which believes that performance is determined by the availability of resources and other characteristics of the organizations they lead.

The individualistic school begins with a discussion of what leadership is. Definitions of leadership suggest:

> leaders will help to define reality for others; they interpret actions, give meaning and perspective to events. (Morley 1984: 269)

> Leadership is to do with forging the meanings which form the bedrock of organizational culture. (Peters and Waterman 1982: 75)

Moreover, there is a shift from discussions of the power and influence of leaders towards an understanding that effective leadership also involves motivation of the people who work in the organization. This view is built into definitions of leadership such as that of Bryman (1986) who argues:

> Leadership entails a sensitivity to the needs and values of followers which implies that it is not simply a matter of doing things to subordinates. (Bryman (1986): 193)

and this involvement of both leaders and followers is also seen in the views of Burns (1978):

> I define leadership as leader inducing followers to act for certain goals that represent the values and motivations – the wants and needs, the aspirations and expectations – of both leaders and followers. (Burns 1978: 19)

The implication of these views is that, to be effective, leaders rely on their followers as well as on their own abilities.

The "contextual" school of leadership goes further, not just looking at the "followers" in the organization, but also arguing that other aspects of the organization itself play an important role in whether the leader will bring about high levels of performance in an organization.

One of the major contributions to the "contextual" school comes from Lieberson and O'Connor (1972), who found evidence that the state of the economy, the industry sector and the relative position of the organization within its sector had a stronger impact on both sales and earnings than did the leader. Lieberson and O'Connor concluded that:

> in emphasizing the effects of leadership we may be overlooking far more powerful environmental influences. Unless leadership is studied as part of a total set of forces, one cannot gauge its impact. (Lieberson and O'Connor 1972: 129)

This view was later supported by other researchers such as Samuelson, Galbraith and McGuire (1985) and Salancik and Pfeffer (1977) whose studies of US mayors found that their effectiveness was heavily influenced by outside interest groups. The contextual view suggests that leadership should be studied in the context of external forces and those which are inside the organization.

Significantly, one of the fields which leans towards support for the "contextual" view of leadership is the sports field. As far back as the 1960s and 1970s, studies such as those by Grusky (1963), Gamson and Scotch (1964), Eitzen and Yetnnan (1972) and Allen, Panian and Lotz (1979), took a contextualist view of leadership in the sports field. Allen, Panian and Lotz studied fifty years of major league baseball data to conclude that leaders were not the only influence on performance. Indeed frequent changes of baseball coach had an adverse effect on performance. Whilst not quite as severe, in American Football, Brown (1982) found neither a positive nor negative effect of changing leader, suggesting that factors other than the leader were the causes of good or poor performance (See Chapter 5 for a fuller discussion of the issues of leadership succession.) This view is supported by recent research into football by Kuper and Szymanski (2009) which argues that the quality of players is the greatest determinant of success in a football club and the rest, even who the manager is, is just "noise."

Later research calls into question Lieberson and O'Connor's (1972) findings – on the basis of the technical details of how they analyzed their data – arguing that they understated the importance of the individual leader on performance (Berkeley Thomas 1988). This "individualist" view may then have more credence that originally thought.

In the light of the debate about the roles of leader, follower and the context of the organization and industry, this chapter begins with a discussion of leadership literature's understanding of the influence of context on leadership effectiveness and presents an in-depth discussion of the context in which football managers work and the challenges which they face.

Leadership: schools of thought

Individualistic approaches

In reviewing leadership theory, Bryman (1989) identifies four main schools of thought:

- The trait approach: up to 1940s.
- Style of leadership: late 1940s to 1960s.
- Contingency approach: late 1960s to early 1980s.
- Transformational leadership: since the early 1980s.

It should be noted that Bryman sees each of these schools of thought as having been replaced by another. In reality, though, there are still recent and valuable studies which have their roots in each of the approaches.

This review begins at the beginning, however. Early individualistic studies of leadership focus on the characteristics of the leader. The *trait approach* to leadership, which dominated until the late 1940s was concerned with what types of people were likely to be good leaders. Bryman (1989) summarizes this approach as follows:

A wide range of diverse personal traits were examined: physical characteristics [such as tall but not too tall]; intelligence and abilities (like verbal fluency); personality characteristics (such as aggressiveness and assertiveness); there were characteristics directly related to tasks, such as achievement drive; and finally researchers looked at social characteristics like cooperativeness, sociability and tact. (Bryman 1989: 35)

From the late 1940s, the emphasis switched towards the *style of leadership*; to how leaders behaved, rather than what they were like. This was mainly because, for every trait that one person argued was important, someone else would suggest that it was not so important and the school began to go round in circles. A characteristic which might be useful in one situation might not be of much use in others.

The move towards studies of the style of leadership in the 1960s looked at types of behavior which motivated employees and resulted in greater effectiveness among the "followers," or members of the organization. The types of behavior which were valued by followers was contrasted with those valued by the leader's superiors. So, while a follower might think it important that the leader be considerate, the superior might place more importance on the ability to be organized. Increasingly, authors began to think that a certain type of behavior might be more important in one situation, whilst another might work better in others. So effective leadership, they argued, is "contingent" on the situation.

Thinking about each of these approaches in relation to football management, a quick mental run through the list of successful football managers, reveals the short and the tall, reflective and flamboyant, autocratic and "one of the lads," as well as meticulous planners and charismatic motivators. Much as early leadership research concludes, there is no one set of characteristics or style which dominates.

There are, however, characteristics and abilities which may be important to the role which a football manager plays – Ronay's (2009) tongue-in-cheek chapter headings for his recent football management book include "The Manager learns to talk," "The Manager learns to swear" and "The manager becomes incredibly famous" as well as the "Dawn of the Showmen." As this would suggest, the spotlight upon the football manager with 24/7 media coverage, the growing global marketplace for football and the intense emotional connection between fans and their clubs means that the football manager will need to embrace the need for a public persona and decide on the way to handle this spotlight. Some managers seem almost to enjoy the cut and thrust with the media, others try to avoid media other than where this relates to the match on Saturday (or Sunday, Monday, Tuesday and whatever other permutations are now possible) and yet others appear uncomfortable with the degree of celebrity – and resultant intrusion which this brings into all aspects of their life.

The characteristics and style of management which might be most important for football managers are discussed later in this chapter based on analysis of interviews with football managers.

As the leadership literature concludes, the particular context in which football managers work may play an important role in the ability to succeed. In other words, success is contingent on doing the right things for the circumstances which surround football managers. This *contingency* approach to leadership gained in popularity from the 1960s onwards. From this perspective, what works for a leader is determined by the specifics of the situation. So, for example, House's "path–goal" theory of leadership (1966) discussed different styles which might work for different types of task and with different types of subordinate. The basis of this work was that leaders are more effective when they fit with the context and motivate employees to believe that their work will provide them with a rewarding outcome. House proposed that if the task was routine and boring then a leader might be most effective in joining in and becoming one of the group "come on lads we're in this together", whereas leadership of a one-off task might work best using an achievement-oriented style ("Let's show them what we can do and win this tournament"). House's path–goal theory of leadership stressed that leaders are more effective when they fit with the context of the organization. House's four styles were:

- **Directive**. This is appropriate if a situation is ambiguous. In this case the role of the leader is to absorb uncertainty for the group. The key task for the leader is to let people know what is expected, to say what should be done and how and to set standards of performance.

- **Supportive**. This might be appropriate if tasks are repetitive. The role of the leader is to guide from within the group: "I am with you in this" "we are in this together let's make the best we can of it." In this situation the key tasks for the leader are to be interpersonally aware of needs of others and to treat the group as equals.
- **Achievement-oriented**. This type of leadership might work for ambiguous, one-off tasks. In this case the challenge is to strive for excellence. The key tasks are to set goals that are challenging and seek continuous improvements. The leader's role in this situation is to emphasize the importance of excellence.
- **Participative**. This leadership style works best with internally oriented people and one-off tasks. Let these people take responsibility for their own performance so that they do not feel patronized. Key tasks: consult others regularly. Ask for suggestions and advice. Take these into account when making decisions.

If this approach were taken to determine what would be effective for a football manager, it is important to define the key tasks and role of the football manager. For example, in some instances, the football side of the club is clearly an operational activity run by a first-team coach. In this case it might well be that the "**supportive**" leadership role identified by House is the most appropriate. The day-to-day coaching side of football presumably contains a good deal of routine and repetition and cannot hope to recreate the excitement of match day so the approach of being close to the players and being involved in the activities with them might well be combined with the role of structuring sessions and providing feedback. If this role is not part of the manager's responsibilities, it might be appropriate for the assistant manager or first-team coach. House suggests that different styles might be adopted alongside each other as appropriate to the task at hand.

It may well be the case, however, that an individual is better suited in character or abilities to one of the styles whilst others are able to adapt and use different styles in different situations. This might well be why some assistant managers – who are incredibly good at working with and understanding players day-to-day – do not easily make the transition to manager. It should be noted that some excellent potential football managers pass through having this responsibility and can also adapt their style to other roles.

The other tasks identified by House might all apply to football to a greater or lesser extent. So, for example, football is certainly uncertain. Football managers have to deal with many matches in close succession, a changing pool of available talent (with injuries and suspensions) and opposition who may play to varying levels, sometimes to the best of their ability and raise their game and others underperforming, together with changing weather and individual and team performances. Certainly the need to offer clear instruction and have a "**directive**" style is one that might seem appropriate to football.

The description of an ambiguous and one-off task sounds like a cup final, play-off final or maybe a series of cup matches which happen at intervals or a football tournament such as the World Cup or European Championships. In keeping with House's suggestions, a football manager in this situation might be exhorting his players to make sure they can be proud of their performance, to enjoy the occasion or to continue to build on the performances of previous rounds. This "**achievement-oriented**" leadership style might work well in this type of situation.

House's final type of task or situation is trickier in that it refers also to the type of individual as well as the nature of the task. For internally oriented individuals (House's example is researchers or scientists) who are involved in a one-off task then the "**participative**" style allows the individual scope to own a problem and to be creative in deciding how best to handle this. It may be that in this case, some of the more introverted characters (or perhaps senior players who have heard it all before and are clear about what the occasion entails) might appreciate more a leadership style which involves them and asks their views, which they can then see being taken into account.

It might be that more than one of these styles is used with different players on the same occasion and that a planned approach is needed to cope with different preferences among the players.

As well as the work of House, other prominent authors in the Contingency school of leadership theory included Vroom and

Yetton (1973) who focused on whether the leader should take an authoritarian, top–down, style of management or a more participative style, which involved others. The authors identified five different styles of leadership:

- Autocratic 1 (A1) Solve problem using information which is already available.
- Autocratic 2 (A2) Obtain additional information from the group before leader makes decision.
- Consultative 1 (C1) The leader makes a decision based on discussing the problem with subordinates individually.
- Consultative (C2) Decisions are made after discussing a problem with the group.
- Group-based (G2) The leader acts as the chair for decisions which are made by the group.

After identifying these different styles, Vroom and Yetton then proposed seven "rules" which might determine which style might work best for the leader. These were written in the style of a decision tree:

Decision quality

- When decision quality is important and the followers possess useful information, then A1 and A2 are not the best method.
- When the leader considers decision quality important but followers do not, then G2 is inappropriate.
- When decision quality is important, the problem is unstructured and the leader lacks either then information or skill to make a decision alone, then G2 is best.

Decision acceptance

When decision acceptance is important and followers are unlikely to accept an autocratic decision, then A1 and A2 are inappropriate.

- When decision acceptance is important but followers are likely to disagree with one another, then A1, A2 and C1 are not appropriate, because they do not give opportunity for differences to be resolved.

- When decision quality is not important but decision acceptance is critical, then G2 is the best method.
- When decision quality is important, all agree with this, and the decision is not likely to result from an autocratic decision then G2 is best.

Whilst these approaches represent a step forward from earlier schools of leadership thought, it is clear that they provide limited insight into more complex situations, personalities of the individuals involved and nuances of how best these styles might be used. It is also inferred that leaders might vary between the different styles in different situations. In practice this is difficult and may be unworkable, although contingency approaches do prompt leaders to start to think about different situations and the challenges that they present.

The shortcomings of contingency approaches to leadership, resulted in a further shift in thinking. This was stimulated by books such as Peters and Waterman's *In Search of Excellence,* which saw leadership as something which "stirred people's emotions and encouraged them to think about possibilities and achievements that would not otherwise have occurred to them." (Bryman 1989: 37)

Transformational leadership believes that successful leaders tend to have clear visions for the direction in which their organizations should go. They pursue this direction with certainty and instil a sense of confidence in those who surround them. Whilst vision, drive and the ability to motivate others are clearly important, Bryman sounds a note of caution. Not all visions and cultures are effective, so how should we recognize those which are effective? Furthermore, there is a danger of "one best way" thinking, which was the difficulty of early leadership studies.

Are visionary leaders and strong cultures relevant to all contexts?

Contextual studies of leadership

When Lieberman and O'Connor (1972) identified the possible limits of the influence of the leader on organizational effectiveness and suggested that context – the outside world, organization and relative position of the organization compared with its competitors – might all influence effectiveness, an alternative field of leadership research began to emerge.

Although critics pointed to flaws in the way in which Lieberman and O'Connor had calculated their results and suggested that looking differently at the data might lend more support for the role of individual leaders, their study set in train a series of other researchers who emphasized the importance of understanding the context of leadership.

In their leadership study, Leavy and Wilson (1994) identified four different organizational contexts which might pose different challenges for the leader. Different leadership styles for different occasions are also described by Ward (2003) who classifies leaders as creator, accelerator, transformer, sustainer and terminator. The latter is used in situations of acquisition or in temporary organizations (for example, the 2012 Olympic Committee which will eventually reach the end of its purpose.) These styles might relate to different stages of the development of organizations. In the football context, the following might be most appropriate:

Builder	Develops something from scratch in the early stages of development.
Revitalizer	Re-energizes in a context where the organization has lost momentum.
Accelerator	Continues and adds momentum to a change process begun by someone else.
Turn-arounder	Involved in major changes in several parts of an organization where several things are going wrong.
Inheritor	Takes over something which is successful and tries to continue the success using own style.

If this were put into the football context, the types of clubs which might fit into each of these situations might be:

Builder:	Clubs who have just come into the football league such as Burton, or newly formed clubs

such as AFC Wimbledon which are built from scratch and rise through the non-league pyramid.

Accelerator: Moving a club on to the next level by promotion. This may require a step change in resources, quality of players. This may be the situation, for example, if a club has been acquired by new owners who invest and want to see the club move forwards rapidly. Examples might include Manchester City, Notts County, Peterborough.

Revitalizer: Just missed out on promotion or playoffs but has the basis of something good on which to build, e.g. Sheffield United, Preston, Millwall or Leeds. May need to shake things up to achieve targets next time round.

Turn-a-rounder: May need to clear out existing players and rebuild squad, possibly backroom and broader organization. Ward refers to this as the "transformer."

Inheritor: Takes over something which is working well, so for example when Sir Alex Ferguson retires from Manchester United and someone else takes over, the new leader's challenge will be to continue the club's success without rocking the boat or becoming a paler shadow of the previous manager. Ward refers to this as the "sustainer."

Some studies go further, arguing that large organizations "run themselves" and that the leader is of little importance (Hall 1972, Cyert and March 1963). Hall says that a leader: "is important in times of organizational growth, development and crisis, but for the most part organizations require maintenance and the organizational leader will make little difference in performance. That is not to say that the presence or absence of top leadership is unimportant, but that the particular incumbent of the leadership position is of little import."

Certainly, Lieberson and O'Connor (1972) found that factors other than the leader played the major role in how well an organization performed. They found that economic conditions and industry and competitive factors had a bigger bearing than anything the leader might do. Based on this, it may well be that in a club with declining attendance and revenue, competing against richer clubs in the same league, the football manager has relatively little bearing on success.

To gain a fuller understanding of the context of football management, and its likely impact on success, the following section reviews previous studies of football management and uses the words of the managers themselves to describe the main challenges of their role.

The world of the football manager: from gaffer to goldfish bowl

Evolution of the role

The role of the football manager has changed dramatically since its earliest days. Green (2002) and, more recently, Ronay (2009) have provided compelling accounts of the evolution of the football manager throughout the professional era of football. This evolution has progressed from the early beginnings in the late nineteenth century when football managers were business managers. Ronay describes this era as follows: "recruiting from the ranks of ex-players was out. At this stage there was no such thing as an ex-player. So managers were sourced from other industries, usually from the senior ranks of manual labour, the factory clerk and the shop steward" (Ronay 2009: 5). Green comments:

> Football managers did precisely what their job title suggested – they managed football clubs. They did not coach the players, they did not don tracksuits or woolly jumpers with whistles round their necks on wobbly bicycles, they did not devise tactics or discuss intricate moves. A trainer, or more probably the team captain did that. Instead the

manager – truly the gaffer of the football factory – wore a suit and ran the administrative affairs of the club from top to bottom. Sometimes he had a secretary, sometimes he didn't. Sometimes he did both jobs. (Green 2002: 47)

As late as the 1970s, some leading football managers fulfilled this type of role, sometimes combining this also with the coaching side of the club so that they truly ran everything. One such manager of the period comments: "I used to run everything. I had to sort out the finances, the wages, the stadium, the pitch and ground staff as well as the coaching and team selection. I even used to organize the Christmas party for all of the staff and their families, not just the football side, everyone."

This central role may play some part in the use of the word "gaffer," a name still used by the players to refer to football bosses. As Green puts it:

no self-respecting overalled worker would ever call a smart-arsed yuppie a gaffer. It just doesn't work. Gaffers ruled ok. People in charge of boats are called old gaffers. Film and Lighting engineers are called gaffers. Dictionaries define gaffers as paternalistic figures, often old men, respected for their wisdom and seniority ... Today the only people who call their bosses gaffers with any hint of sincerity are footballers, sometimes even foreign footballers for whom the phrase has no significance. (Green 2002: 28–9)

In the 1970s, Ronay (2009) assesses the football manager as being "indisputably in charge" but in charge in a football industry which was

an industry in the middle of twenty years of sullen decline. The decay in football's infrastructure had become chronic. Ancient stadia groaned and leaked. Concrete terraces crumbled. Football smelled of mildew and wet rot ... at the same time the atmosphere around it had become hostile. Assorted firms and crews spent their Saturdays trashing the nation's railway carriages, terrorising the nation's bus-stops and dragging football in a jeering headlock through a succession of provincial town centres (Ronay 2009: 172)

He references the question posed by the title of Brian Glanville's *1974 Soccer Gift Book*: "Has Football a Future?"

It is too easy now to forget, in the light of the massive development of football as a game and as a global business, the concern was serious. These crumbling stadia, incipient unrest among supporters or policing of fans by those who expected it, would result in a number of football stadium tragedies in the 1980s including Bradford, Heysel and Hillsborough.

In the aftermath, football became, in the words of Ward and Williams (2009), quite literally "a whole new ball game." The official enquiry into the Hillsborough disaster led by Lord Justice Taylor resulted in a report which demanded all-seater stadia and better conditions and safety for supporters but also; "a totally new approach across the whole field of football (requiring) higher standards both in bricks and in human relations" (Taylor Report 1990).

Gilmore says "it could be argued that the major outcome was a reorientation of football as an object of consumption." (2001: 125). Football shifted its focus. Stadia became venues for family entertainment. The FA, under the leadership of Graham Kelly, unveiled its "Blueprint for Football" on 20 June 1991 and proposed "a Premier League within the administration of the Football Association." This was to contain at least twelve clubs including the big five of Manchester United, Arsenal, Liverpool, Everton and Tottenham Hotspur. In 1992, the Premier League was launched with 22 teams. The remaining 70 clubs remained in the Football League. Also central to the Blueprint were more marketing and commercial activities by the FA. These would generate income from which clubs could fund stadium improvements and the creation of all-seater stadia.

Indeed Williams suggests that "the new league was created by and for television" (Williams 1996: 10).

With this commercialization, came new challenges for the role of football manager. As football clubs have transmogrified into businesses, they have developed more typical business structures. They may now have a Chief Executive or Chief Operating Officer, non-Executive Directors, PR staff, press officers and Finance, Marketing and other functional Directors. Sometimes they have a Director of Football – although the responsibilities of this role also vary club to club from a Board-level "Sporting Director" type of role, to player recruitment, to a split of responsibilities with the football manager at operational level. In training and preparing football players for the role of football manager, capturing the range of structures, strategies and systems is complex.

Despite all the changes, in contrast to the European model of Sporting Director and Head Coach, where the business aspects of the football operation are run by the former and the training of the players by the latter, English clubs still often combine the role of first team coach or trainer with the manager. The English football manager, unlike his European opposite number, is a broad football and administrative role where the manager identifies, negotiates and signs the players who will make up his team.

Football managers are still gaffer to their players, football interviews and conversations are full of "and I said gaffer" "and I told the gaffer" comments, but the nature of the role has changed radically. They may think of themselves as having taken on the role of football manager in the mold of the managers who influenced their own playing careers. Yet the context in which they manage has shifted such that there are fundamental differences in what is expected and demanded of them.

A young manager commented to me:

> What strikes me most about being a football manager now is the shift in power. Even at the top end – and don't get me wrong someone like Sir Alex Ferguson is massively influential – but I bet even he has noticed a shift in power over the time he has been manager at Manchester United. Decisions now are not always made by the manager but by the Chairman and Board of Directors, be that at a top end PLC or a lower league club with an overzealous Chairman and Board who think they know a lot about football. From what they say, football managers used to have pretty much a "carte blanche" to do what they wanted, bring in players and make decisions. Now the players have more power, the supporters can air their views via the internet or on radio phone-in immediately after a match. Every aspect is gone into in the nth degree. Before, even if a result had gone badly, the manager wouldn't have had to face the fans until the next week. Now the fans have their say straight away.

In contrast, in 2000, one of Gilmore's football manager respondents said:

> I don't think Directors know exactly what the job is … they're
> all great with hindsight … some let you get on with it … but
> I wouldn't tolerate a lot of interference. Either I'm running
> it and if my head's on the block I'm not having people tell
> me what to do. I'm prepared to listen, but if I'm making the
> decision, its mine.

The seeming contradiction in these two views, one from a more
experienced and one from a younger manager perhaps reflects a
transition in the football manager's role even in recent times. Or
perhaps it highlights one of the biggest challenges facing football
managers: that of a further shift in the role of football manager.

Many owners want to take control away from the football
manager, either because they consider themselves to be business
experts who want to control finances, because they come from
countries where they are used to a Sporting Director and Head
Coach model of football club management or else perhaps because
they are, by origin, fans – who like all fans secretly believe that
they could select and recruit a winning team. The traditional
football manager then becomes more of a Head Coach as in the
European system. In the eyes of the fans and media, though, acc-
ountability lies with the manager rather than the Board.

There are numerous possible explanations for football managers getting a hard time from fans. Perhaps fans do not realize that
the roles and responsibilities have changed. Or maybe they have
unrealistic expectations of where the club should be. It could be
that they don't understand the realities of football finance in the
current era. Many times, fans ring into radio shows and post on
web-boards comments such as "we pay our money and we have
a right to …" or "with our level of support we should be pushing
for …" In reality, though, in the English Premier league match-
day revenue accounts for only an average of 13 percent of total
revenue, a small proportion of the outlay on player wages. Below
the Premier League, most clubs make an operating loss and managers are often operating under severe financial constraints whilst
facing pressure to improve the performance of the team.

Even where the difficulties are fairly clear, as recently with Darlington FC's administration, the manager may be given little leeway. Colin Todd lasted only nine games into the current season before being dismissed and commented that this was always likely in a results business (Darlington and Stockton Times 26 September 2009).

Two clashes, those of Kevin Keegan and Alan Curbishley with the Boards of Newcastle United and West Ham United respectively, seem to have resulted from different expectations of the roles and responsibilities of the football manager. The LMA statement at the time of Alan Curbishley's resignation from West Ham United said:

> Alan Curbishley has today resigned as manager of West Ham United, a position he had held since December 2006. The club's unilateral actions around player transfers, without reference to their manager, have created irreparable damage to Alan's working relationship with the directors. He said: "I started my West Ham United career when I left school in 1974 and have remained a lifelong fan. I have been incredibly proud to manage such a great club and my decision to resign has been very tough. The selection of players is critical to the job of the manager and I had an agreement with the club that I alone would determine the composition of the squad. However, the club continued to make significant player decisions without involving me. In the end such a breach of trust and confidence meant that I had no option but to leave. Nevertheless, I wish the club and the players every success in the future." (http://www.leaguemanagers.com/news/viewfromthetop-6169.html 3 September 2008)

On his departure from Newcastle United, the LMA website gave the following statement from Kevin Keegan:

> I've been working desperately hard to find a way forward with the directors, but sadly that has not proved possible. It's my opinion that a manager must have the right to manage and that clubs should not impose upon any manager any player that he does not want. It remains my fervent wish to see Newcastle United

do well in the future and I feel incredibly sorry for the players, staff and most importantly the supporters. I have been left with no choice other than to leave. (http://www.leaguemanagers.com/news/viewfromthetop-6170.html, 4 September 2008)

In some club structures, there are different perspectives and understanding of the role of the football manager. Understandably, as the manager is hired and – very often – fired on the basis of his players' performance, many managers feel that they want to control all aspects of the resources with which they work, whom they sign, what type of player and whether the player fits with their vision of success.

A clear understanding of what the football manager's role is seems vital to building a successful relationship between the two parties. Moreover, it seems that football managers are presented with incredible challenges and are judged on their ability to achieve these in a timescale in which it is not clear that any manager, no matter how experienced, talented or successful would be able to deliver the required performance.

In her football management research, Gilmore (2000) uses the following description of the football manager's job, as explained to her by one of her football manager interviewees:

I would say it's the preparation of a team and the building of a team … to compete against people trying to do the same as you and you're trying to do it better than them in order to win more matches than you lose and that's it and it encompasses the actual direct preparation of the team for a game to be played on the Saturday and the longer-term preparation of it through accumulating the best players you can to do the job that you've got to do.

At the bottom line, this **is** the football manager's job. When interviewed, football managers will sometimes go back to saying "my job is to win football matches" as a defence against being drawn into broader discussion of what might be happening off the pitch. So when Paul Hart, manager of Portsmouth was interviewed on television after winning his first Premier League match of the season, interviewers were more interested in discussing the non-payment of players, possible new takeover of the club and illness of the prospective owner rather than his success in winning the match.

Here is the crux of the challenge facing a football manager. The manager is increasingly the visible face of the club. He tends to hold a press conference before each match to discuss the game. As football clubs become ever higher profile, however, and as many have press officers adept at handling press, the manager who voluntarily holds a regular press conference before a match, or is interviewed afterwards, is an excellent source of information on the club in general. To some extent the football manager is pushed into acting as the voice of the club.

Yet if a manager does make a comment about the club more broadly, it is possible that they will be accused by the club of overstepping the parameters of their job.

The world of today's football manager

Football is a tough game. Peter Taylor took Wycombe Wanderers up a divison and yet was sacked ten games into the new season. John Barnes was given eleven games at Tranmere before his dismissal.

Many issues may impact on the football manager's ability to deliver results. The context at each club is different. It may be that the manager has to cope with injuries, a new league, tough finances – many clubs need to cut budgets in the current difficult financial climate – it may also be that managers have different personalities and skills which make them better or less able to cope with the challenges of being a manager:

> There are both external and internal parts of being successful as a football manager. The external things include having good players, the fans being behind you, having the financial backing. You may be able to influence these things but often they are outside your control. The internal aspects are those personal qualities of vision, preparation for the job, ability to plan ahead, charisma and determination. Notwithstanding the fact that the most successful people make their own, luck is also a big factor.

Whilst Chairmen and managers might know the realities of what goes into forming a squad and keeping the club in a healthy financial position, this may not always be fully realized or appreciated by fans and media, and the pressure of failing to challenge for titles and promotions may be heaped onto the manager. The importance of the club's finances in determining what level of performance is realistic is highlighted by Deloitte & Touche's *Annual Review of Football Finance* (2009). The quality of the squad – as measured by how much players are paid – has a direct relationship with on-the-pitch success, particularly in the premier league.

The football manager might – quite literally – be living their life in the fast lane. They could be juggling many different tasks, doing their own scouting at reserve fixtures up and down the country, travelling to and from matches without the resources to book a flight or hotel – with long coach journeys and late nights. Here, in their own words, and based on previous research into football managers, is their assessment of the life of a football manager.

Specialists and generalists

At higher levels, a club might have a whole team of football backroom staff; a manager, an assistant manager, a first-team coach, masseur, data analyst, nutritionist, physio, sports scientist, kitman and so on. Here the manager, like in any business, has to make sure everyone is clear about their roles, set the strategy and plans and oversee what is going on. Lower down the leagues, the football manager might be doing most of these things himself – I've known football managers who are paying the hotel bills out of their own pocket, driving young players to matches, got loan players staying at their house, or maybe do everything with one or two staff. Then everyone has two or more things they're responsible for and they need to be able to be flexible and do whatever jobs come up.

The role of the football manager varies significantly depending on the level and resources of the club and the way in which it is structured. Generally speaking, the lower down the league structure, and the tighter the finances, the more the football manager will need to be a multi-talented juggler – trying to source masseurs, physios and other necessary skills from local universities, even negotiating with councils and schools to find a pitch to train on. Higher up the league structure, the manager might not be doing everything himself, he may have a team of staff whom he manages.

It is easy to assume, because the roles are very different, that perhaps different types of managers would be better suited to each. Certainly, managing lower down the leagues has its challenges, it's a hard job, long hours, it might be frustrating and the salary is much lower than many people would believe. Managers, in moments of frustration, express the view that football management may be "undoable" because the expectations are unrealistically high, the pressure is on to get consistently high performance from the players week in, week out. And if the manager does all of this, then next season the Chairman and fans will expect even more. Yet most managers, even when they have been sacked and suffered the pain would come back and do it all again because it is in their blood:

> People say "I would defy Sir Alex Ferguson or Arsène Wenger or any of those top managers to manage in this situation". But people forget that they – the top managers – have been there. They have done that. They have managed on small budgets. They started right at the lowest level, learned their trade. Look at the clubs they worked in – Arsène Wenger, Alex Ferguson, Sven Göran Eriksson. They haven't just got there overnight. They have had a long journey and reached the top of their trade. People tend to forget.

Football managers do face different challenges at different levels. In fact every situation is different, every club. The quality of the infrastructure, stadium, size of the average crowd and revenue, as well as the relative quality of the squad differ within, as well as between, leagues. There is no reason why the manager who manages at the top level should be viewed as essentially different to the football manager lower in the league structure. Certainly, it is worth considering what the differences might be. This is a two-way street. Prospective football managers who played at higher levels may be unused to the level of the players, club facilities, grounds in which they have to play and even styles of play in different leagues. Those who played and learned their trade at lower levels will have to learn how to deal with the larger teams of specialists, higher expectations and brighter spotlights which are part and parcel of clubs which play at higher levels.

Life in the fast lane

The life of the football manager has been likened to driving down the fast lane of a motorway with your foot down. Constantly rushing to watch matches, opponents and promising players, on the phone – hands free – or phones – many managers have more than one phone, setting out early in the morning, getting home late at night or not at all. Not always eating healthily, eating at the wrong times, too little time to devote to family, friends, their own fitness.

Let there be no doubt, the life of a football manager is hard. And many managers believe that it is getting harder:

> It does seem to be getting harder. No matter how well you do in the Football League you don't always get the chance to manage at the higher levels. People used to do their apprenticeship in the lower leagues and get their experience and, if they did well, they would move up the leagues. But that doesn't always seem to happen now. Someone might manage for their whole career at the lower league level.

> I believe there is a massive over-expectation. It is at epidemic proportions throughout football. By definition this means you are going to be viewed as a failure because you can't achieve what is expected, even if it is unrealistic. Often it is short-termist. We need success now. You don't have time to build anything. The timescales on which people are judged are so short. A manager might get a season, half a season, ten games, even less. Then we decide that they are a good or bad manager.

If the fans lash out when the team loses, it may be that the manager is suffering no less:

> You have to deal with the disappointment of losses. You might lose matches, you might lose key players, your backroom staff and eventually your job. You have to be able to deal with those things, otherwise don't be a football manager.

It is a long job. You work such long hours. If you lose it is a horrible, a horrible journey back. You might have arrangements to go out, but that is all off. You don't feel like it. Sometimes I don't want to talk about it. I just want to get away on my own.

There are many affirmations of how much it hurts to lose in football managers' accounts in the press and in their biographies. They might not want to go out on a Saturday if the result goes against them. If they lose, just don't talk to them, particularly if it was to a disputed penalty or a last minute defensive error. What someone else might accept graciously, the competitive person will struggle with. What made them a winner as a player – competitive spirit, a will to win – might mean that they find it difficult to lose at anything.

Monitoring the heart rates of football managers during matches shows the physical, and very real, dangers of the pressures that football managers are under. This was revealed in shocking detail in a BBC *Tonight* programme in 2002 when heart monitoring of Dave Bassett and Sam Allardyce showed that they both were exposing themselves to very real health risks by the amount of pressure they were under. During a Bolton – Leicester draw in 2001–02, both managers experienced considerable increases in their blood presure. Dave Bassett even showed an irregular heart rate ("The heart of the matter", http://news.bbc.co.uk/sport1/hi/football/1758132.stm, 13 January 2002).

John Barnwell, CEO of the League Managers Association at the time of this research, commented that the intensity of the football manager's role is enormous and claustrophobic. Managers can never get away from the job, it is with them all the time and the danger is that something this all consuming can get in the way of managers looking after themselves.

One of the major challenges for football managers is that of managing expectations among a diverse set of stakeholders who may not all want the same things:

If the club is expected to challenge for honours or promotion and has the funds to back it up, then on the pitch you have to get pretty close to delivering. The bits of luck with squad management i.e injuries either way, can be excused if you go pretty close to that.

For teams expected to be mid-table or lower its a different challenge. There it's about attempting to punch above your weight. Perhaps you can have a cup run to gain some extra money and raise spirits of the fans. This can also help the manager because it has the bonus of raising yours and the club's profile which brings media and other benefits.

Obviously, to be counted as being in any way successful, you've got to get the staff, media and Board of Directors on your side and pulling in the same direction. It isn't always possible and sometimes you can't please all the people and all of those groups, but if you've got most of them onside, the rest normally fall into line.

Life in the goldfish bowl

We tend to believe that managing at higher levels with better resources and infrastructure is easier, but remember:

The spotlight is more intensive at the higher level, more media attention, dealing with far more talented players, who might need more attention. The best players might ask the most questions: how are they going to handle a game? That's how they get to the top. They have the ability, perhaps you can show them once and they will be true professionals and next game they will do what you say, but the more money there is in the club, the higher the expectations and the more the attention.

Successful football managers need to be able to deal with public scrutiny. Every gesture is captured and examined in as much detail as the match itself to see if the manager looks like he is under pressure. Is he angry, how did he react to a penalty decision? At a recent match, Ipswich Town manager Roy Keane allegedly had more cameras pointed at him than were pointed at the players on the pitch.

Ronay (2009) describes the new media profile and how the portrayal of the football manager by the media could raise them either to the role of the Messiah or the Whipping Boy. Discussing the daily pillorying of Graham Taylor during his time as England Manager, he comments:

> For three years Taylor was daily fodder for the red-tops. He was also the first England manager to feature regularly on *Spitting Image,* a weekly fixture of the slate-grey John Major years. Even this provided a flavour of Taylor's status as national whipping boy. His voice on the show was provided by Alistair McGowan, who would occasionally take the puppets out onto the street to gauge public reaction. "We'd taken Jean-Paul Gaultier out, and people had been friendly." McGowan recalled. "But then we took Graham Taylor into the Coach and Horses in Soho. And this bloke said, 'Oi, Taylor, come here: you are a disgrace. I don't know how you got the job. You should go now'... It was amazing, the vitriol I got on Graham's behalf. If that's what the puppet gets, what does Taylor get in person?" (Ronay 2009: 212)

There is a sense that, even when the response of fans and media is less dramatic that it was for Graham Taylor, that the success or failure of a manager might be affected not only by what they actually do, but by how they are portrayed in the media:

> How would a lower league manager fare managing at the top level? Well we have had some great young British managers getting a taste of it – Alan Pardew, Aidy Boothroyd, Phil Brown – and they have done very well with what they had. I think more people could make the step up. The two or three core skills are the same – identify the players, bring the best out of them, get them to deliver the results on the day. But sometimes we don't get behind them. As soon as there is a bad run of results people shoot them down. You can be built up quickly, but you can be back down their just as quickly.

> Its what they have read in the papers. The paper will go "oh this man's a tactical genius ... and I think 'is this the bloke I know and go out for a drink with? ... Directors read these papers and they say 'this manager? Yes he's a tactical genius.' They haven't got a ... clue." (Gilmore 2000: 167)

Talent management

Overall I think the recruitment of key staff and of course players
has to be high on the list of what it takes to be successful as a
football manager!

What does a football manager need to do to succeed? Find
and sign good players for your team. An essential part of the
process is who you get in your line up. Find them, recruit
them, determine the tactics and manage them in a way that
will get the best out of them. Sounds easy doesn't it?

Gilmore describes the way in which a football manager often
sees himself as a father figure:

The moment I took over as manager I said to all the players,
"if you've got any problems, just come and see me, that's what
I am here for" ... I like to think of myself as a father figure.
I also like to think that I was there for the staff to come and
say if they had any problems. (Gilmore 2000: 183)

Whether in fact the manager is a "father-figure," a more nurturing almost "mother" to the players (as suggested by Gilmore),
or a counsellor to the players, it is clear that building a team of
talented individuals and getting the best out of them on a regular
basis is one of the key challenges facing the football manager.

Furthermore, dealing with talented football players, particularly at higher levels where the wealth of these individuals
may far exceed that of the manager, is not always plain sailing.
Mechanisms that might work in most business settings – monetary
sanctions and rewards for example – might not be sufficient to
motivate these players to behave in certain ways. Indeed, if there
is a shortage of talent and a variety of interested clubs, power
might lie with the player (and their chosen representative) and the
contract may do little to tie the player to the club.

Yet life within a football club may not always be easy for
players. In his book on professional footballers, Martin Roderick
(2006) shows all too clearly the fear that players may have if
they feel that they will not be retained, the rejection they feel
if out injured for a length of time and no longer part of the

group. Whilst some players might need a manager to put them in their place, others might need an arm round them. Particularly for young players, football banter can seem intimidating:

> There is a football mentality … you have to be a footballer to appreciate it … there is a football humour … within dressing rooms and … it can be cruel. You have to be able to handle that.
>
> Most footballers, as my wife will tell you, have the same sense of humour. We're all like peas out of the same pod … we have our different personalities but our sense of humour is virtually the same … I think it's just the dressing room mentality – the banter that goes on … a lot of dressing room banter is a lot of mickey-taking, a lot of character building. (Gilmore 2000: 187).

Football is not alone in this. Socialization – becoming part of the group, proving that you can "take it" – is common to many sectors. Graduate trainees, media, financial workers in the City have all commented on the need to be able to burn the candle at both ends, to start at the bottom, make the tea and fetch the sandwiches, or the jibes and tricks which may go with initiation.

The manager may have to be removed from the banter, but learn when to join in. Being part of, or at least aware of, the banter gives him insights into what is going on with the mood of his players. He also needs to judge when someone may be struggling. There are countless stories of homesick youngsters and those who may be lacking confidence or otherwise suffering, but feel unable to admit it in this "macho" setting.

The team may also be made up of "artists" and "soldiers." The latter might be the mainstay of the team. Those who you would want alongside you in the trenches, consistent, passionate, committed to the cause. Paradoxically, however, the individual creative player, the talented genius, even those who have a dark side and are difficult to manage, may also play an important role in the team. It might be near on impossible to omit the player who can get you a goal, the crowd pleaser, even if they are a poor trainer and otherwise behave in ways which are counter-productive to building a cohesive team.

Teams of talented football players are now, and increasingly, multinational teams. Modern day Premier League teams may be made up of as many different nationalities as there are players. This doesn't just mean that communication is an issue. Football may be a common language, a common passion, but the language issue will be compounded by different cultures, religions, backgrounds and expectations of how football should be played. Already football managers need to view everyone in their team as an individual for whom different approaches might be needed to make them flourish but here multicultural understanding might be asked of football managers who have never played or worked outside of the UK. It may take time for the players to adapt to the country, but also to the style, pace and intensity of the football.

Particular challenges for a football manager lie in:

Identifying talent

This is the most commonly cited ability which football managers consider they need for their role. At different levels, this might mean travelling the length of the country to spot raw talent missed by other managers, countless evenings at reserve matches, or else creating a network of scouts domestically and internationally, who will provide reliable information on the ability, consistency and attitude of players.

There have been several recent discussions about who should be responsible for the identification and signing of players. This is allegedly at the root of the resignations of both Kevin Keegan and Alan Curbishley, who are used to the traditional English model of football management and wish to sign the players on whose performance their abilities will be judged. In other systems, however, this might be the responsibility of a Sporting Director rather than the football manager – who acts more as the Head Coach, getting the best out of players once they are there.

The ability to identify talented individuals is esteemed by football managers. So, for example, Sir Alex Ferguson says of his former captain Steve Bruce, now Sunderland manager, that the latter has an excellent scouting network in areas which other managers don't always look in and the ability to spot players such as John Mensah, Lorik Cana and Wilson Palacios. He also refers to the associated ability to improve these players once they are playing in the English game (*Daily Mail*, "Alex Ferguson: Steve Bruce has the badge of a scout master," 3 October 2009).

Motivating and retaining talent

Although many managers rue their lack of resources to buy the players they want, having all the resources that anyone could want and the ability to assemble a squad of talented individuals still has its challenges:

- Who would be in your best line-up?
- How do you motivate those who aren't in your line-up?
- If you rotate your squad, how does that affect individuals who may see this as a reflection on their performance in the last game?
- What happens if your second-best player for a position could be a competitors' first choice?

Since Russian Oligarch, Roman Abramovitch, invested in Chelsea, there have been several football managers at the club. Whilst some of these have departed by choice – Guus Hiddinck chose to take the role until the end of last season – others, such as Ranieri, Mourinho and Scolari were dismissed. Already in the early days of the 2009–10 season, commentators are pointing to the fact that Chelsea have lost the occasional game and contrasting that with the barnstorming form of Chelsea in previous seasons.

This highlights a number of issues. First, Claudio Ranieri had just under four seasons in charge (2000–04), Mourinho just over three seasons (2004–07), Scolari was in charge for only six months of the 2008–09 season and Hiddinck was only available for part of a season because of his international commitments. Overall therefore, Chelsea's football management has seen rates of change similar to those in clubs with lower levels of resources.

Second, the levels of performance which saw Ranieri, Mourinho and Scolari dismissed were very high, but not considered to be high enough given the quality of the players with whom they were working. Nothing but winning the league and probably also European competition would be counted as success.

Third, despite massive investment, Chelsea did not immediately sweep all before them. Sustained success requires infrastructure, culture and winning ethos which may take time to build. Teams take time to gel together and a collection of talented individuals will not necessarily perform at the expected level when combined. There may be clashes of ego, cultural differences, decisions on who is the best in each position. Based on his frequent squad rotation – and alleged inability to decide on his best line-up – Ranieri was nicknamed "Tinkerman." A top player – particularly one used to being the "star" player, or worried about his place in an international squad – may not be content only to start the occasional match.

Fourth, sustained success requires not just a one-off high investment, but continual investment to keep up with competitors who also have deep pockets. Top players may also still prefer to join a club with a history of success rather than a challenger. Depending on the level of the challenger this may make it difficult to attract the best players. A top player has choices and might be swayed by the international reputation of the club, whether or not it is already competing in Europe and how full the trophy cabinet is, rather than future potential.

Some clubs will openly state that they have a policy on how many players they should have for each position – so for example this is sometimes three, two challengers and one up-and-coming player. If this is achieved, then managers face the difficulty of keeping happy those players who know that they are second or third choice. The danger is that these players may wish to move in order to become someone else's first choice player.

Deciding when to let go ...

Bolchover and Brady (2002) suggest that the best approach may be to view decisions on retaining or letting go of talent as being like a stream, or river. It might be best not simply to dam the stream but to decide when to let that stream take its course. Some of the decisions which are made might appear – at the time – to be surprising, particularly if a football manager sells a player at the top of their game. Sir Alex Ferguson shows masterly judgment of when to let a player go. He released Hughes, Ince, Beckham and Ronaldo to name but a few. These seemed surprising decisions at the time, but sometimes such moves show a shrewd ability to get a good return on a player at the top – rather than selling after their value declines – and can provide resources to buy players to cover other shortages and or allow other younger players to come through. Conversely, some teams never recover from the loss of a player or players who were not even recognized as pivotal at the time:

> Financially if we wanted to sign players I was told that I needed to sell some of the fringe players. They weren't getting many games so I agreed. But one or two characters, I didn't realize until they'd gone that they were a key part of the banter, or they sorted out the music or added to the team spirit and so, even though they weren't our best players, the team lost something once they were no longer there.

Of course, current financial constraints mean that many clubs sign loan players on a short-term basis who can prove to be invaluable. Basing a team on loan players poses different challenges, as these players can be recalled early and there is a need to perpetually reinvent and resettle the team as players come and go. For any team, however, letting even one player go, even if there is someone waiting in the wings to step in as a replacement, can result in a period of readjustment before the team delivers peak performance.

Managing upwards

As well as relationships with players, the football manager must also build and maintain good relationships with the Board, investors and other stakeholders. Football managers generally accept the importance of these "hire and fire" relationships:

> The relationship between the football manager and the Chairman is the most important relationship in football.
>   I worked with one Chairman who was like a father figure. He helped me to understand the finances and other parts of the

club which I hadn't come across before. We are still in touch even though I have moved on from the club.

Of course relationships between manager and Chairman do not always run this smoothly! Gilmore talks about the need for managers to understand the type of structure and where the political power lies in a club:

> Some clubs have too democratic a Board. They talk and talk and talk but no one has the power to go and get it done. Whereas at this club, for example, you know, provided he knows about it, you'll get it done. He has the say. It's not always the best way, but at least you'll get it done. (Gilmore 2000: 165)

> The political skill is to be able to count to 10. It's a very hurtful game. There are things that you don't like, people say things you're sensitive to. People make nasty comments and sometimes on purpose and they can goad you and it's very dangerous … you're on a knife edge all the time and it's very easy to explode, so you've got to count to 10 and you've got to be calm. (Gilmore: 166)

The complexity of the web of relationships surrounding the manager is often mentioned by football managers:

> The key challenge is dealing with the agendas of significant others, i.e players, staff, directors, fans, media and so on. All of the different stakeholders might have conflicting agendas which the manager is surrounded by and he has to try and negotiate a way through which will suit everyone.

Building a backroom team

> I think it is really important that you choose the right number two. You need to choose someone who isn't a yes man. It might be that they are different to you in personality. Someone you

trust, but someone who would pull you up if they think that you are doing or saying the wrong thing. It used to be that people always brought in their mate. It is essential that you trust the person, but you'd be better to bring in the person you think is right for the job rather than someone just because you get on with them. Maybe you like people because they are like you. They might not be the best person for the job, and because you've done them a favour in bringing them in, they might not want to upset you if they disagree.

Being an assistant manager is either great or immensely frustrating depending on your personality. If you're happy playing the junior role, it may be because you love coaching and that's what you are responsible for and that's where you function best. If the manager coaches, maybe you are happy being perhaps the wiser, older counsel. But if you see yourself as a "manager-in-waiting", then as an assistant it's only natural that – if you don't get to make the final decision on tactics or team selection – no matter how loyal you are, it can be frustrating. Whatever the circumstances, the make up of the management team should cover all the bases so that the manager should select his assistant on the basis that the assistant does some of the things he can't do or isn't comfortable doing.

It is easy to think of the football manager in isolation. Indeed it is a lonely role and football managers sometimes reflect on this, particularly when results go against them. Showing any lack of certainty might be viewed as a weakness – and cannot be done in front of the players (don't want to make them worry), staff (don't want to them to think I can't handle it) or Chairman (I will be sacked).

In many cases, however, the football manager does work with a set of other football specialists – the backroom staff. Many managers argue that the choice of these staff, as a sounding board and for the complementary skills which they may have to offer, is essential to the success of the football manager.

Whilst some people argue that being a good "number two" or assistant manager is a career in itself – and some are better suited in temperament or abilities to that role – this may also be a career step along the path to football manager. So a prospective football manager might go into a club to work as an assistant manager to gain experience of coaching and insights into football management. Some ex-football managers gain re-employment as assistant managers, and others will yo-yo back and forth between the two roles rather than pursuing a career solely as one or the other.

The choice of an assistant manager, which was traditionally a trusted mate from playing days, is increasingly someone who is recruited on the basis of having the skills necessary for the role. As football management becomes more pressurized, the assistant – as someone who can take on some parts of the role – is ever more important.

There is no one style of assistant manager. The title was used recently at Watford for Keith Burkinshaw, a vastly experienced former manager who worked alongside Aidy Boothroyd when he was in his first management role. Assistant manager might also be a coaching role equivalent to first team or head coach, but could also be a more administrative role sitting alongside the manager. The role is ideally determined by the manager to be whatever he finds most useful.

Passion and resilience

A recurrent topic in interviews with football managers is that of what makes a winner in football management. There is no one way of succeeding as a football manager – it is clear that a mental run through of the extroverts and introverts, larger than life characters, autocrats, deep thinkers and almost reclusive characters who have made their mark in the game soon makes this clear. Proponents of visionary leadership (or transformational leadership as it is often called in academic literature), however, point to common characteristics such as passion, resilience and will to win. These attributes are equally important in football as for other types of leader.

Passion for the game might be exhibited in the sort of enthusiasm which kept Sir Bobby Robson managing into his seventies;

the drive and competitive spirit which keeps Sir Alex Ferguson wanting to win every game and a sheer inability to stay away from a game recently described by Arsène Wenger.

Among the tributes to Sir Bobby Robson, a number of attributes were described by his fellow managers and admirers; his gentlemanly, dignified and diplomatic behavior (Gary Lineker, BBC Website, 21 September 2009), ability to make friends wherever he went and, perhaps most frequently mentioned of all, his enthusiasm, energy and sense of humor (Sir Alex Ferguson in *The Times* 31 July 2009) and passion and knowledge of the game.

A passion for what they do is inherent in many great leaders. In talking about his football mentor Sir Alex Ferguson, Steve Bruce reflects that he was driven and was a winner and wanted his players to show the same hunger and desire to win that he did (Rob Stewart, *The Telegraph*, 1 October 2009.)

A similar passion can be seen in Arsène Wenger, talking about the possibility of retirement when he recently turned 60 years old. Sky Sports (25 September 2009) comments that he originally thought that he might retire at fifty, but now at sixty appreciates that his life without football would be "unthinkable" and that he will now continue as long as his health and strength permit.

Whilst the personality of the leader is a vital part of success, the characters and styles of those who make successful football managers bear little relation to each other. The rules and strictness of Capello, the calmness of Eriksson, the genial father figure of Sir Bobby Robson. Extrovert or introvert, passionate motivator or reflective student of the game, all of these have worked.

One personality trait which may, however, be of use to the football manager is that of persistence, and perhaps also resilience in the face of adversity. As one manager describes it:

No matter what happens in a match, whether you concede in the last minute to a disputed penalty or whether you lost and were just plain awful, you probably still have another match in a couple of days. I usually go quiet for a day or so, try to do something else and then I think "and we go again …" and we pick ourselves up and start again.

Another attribute which seems to help is confidence:

> I sometimes think that the most successful managers are the
> ones who are really confident in their own ability. Sometimes
> I start out thinking that what I am doing is right, but it takes a
> lot to hold onto your beliefs, especially if results aren't going
> your way. You may be playing well and not having the luck,
> or else it just hadn't quite come together yet, but you have to
> believe in yourself. It can be tough when people start saying
> you are wrong. Football managers need thick skin …

Conclusion

Organizations need leaders. The above discussion shows that, in
football management as in other sectors, the football manager's
job – and chances of success – may be heavily influenced by factors in the context. In particular having the money to buy good
players plays an important part, as does having clearly defined
roles and responsibilities in the club's structure and a shared set
of aims and values.

Leadership theory identifies distinct schools of thought and
different views prevailed in different eras. The reality of football
management lends some support to several of the different views
of leadership. Context does play a role; football managers work
in a world in which they face similar challenges to those facing
managers in many businesses – a preoccupation with results, a
tendency to be short-termist, competition for the best talent,
debates about how to develop and retain talented individuals, the
need to get these talented individuals to work together in a team
and deliver on "match-day."

They also have a set of challenges which are distinctive.
Sometimes these are distinctive because of their intensity. Many
leaders work under public scrutiny. Their results may be publicly
available or reported in the press but few will have to handle the
glare of the spotlight which faces football managers, particularly
at the highest levels.

Leaders in other sectors may be judged on results. Few, however, are judged in quite such a short timescale as the handful of

matches that may be granted a football manager to succeed, nor have their every move, mistake or grimace replayed on television or discussed on websites. They do not tend to face quite the level of public vitriol which might face football managers if results go against them. Some managers dare not even leave their homes after a poor result. Conversely a good result might bring such adulation that the manager cannot go out for a meal with their families without devoted fans continually asking for autographs and photographs.

Many managers from other sectors see themselves reflected in the challenges facing football managers. They may have similar issues in terms of:

- Resource constraints
- Talent wars
- Choosing optimal line-up
- Getting a performance from a team of talented individuals
- Keeping the "reserves" motivated
- Deciding when to let key players leave and at what price
- Being held accountable for results in the short-term whilst trying to build towards long-term success

The remainder of this book accepts that organizations do need leaders. The context may define the challenges that they face and even affect the chances that they will succeed, but this does not take away from the need to study the issues that face leaders.

CHAPTER 3

The Golden Boys: What is Success as a Football Manager and What Influences It?

Introduction

In the Introduction and in Chapter 1, football is described as a "results business." Success might seem easy to define, although different measures are popularly used and results alone may be over-simplistic, ignoring differences in quality of the players – or other influences which might constrain the level of success which is possible.

This chapter begins by reviewing some of the most commonly used measures of success in football and by identifying the strengths and weaknesses of these. It then uses some of these measures to show the issues which arise when trying to compare managers on the basis of simple results – should a manage who achieved this over an extended period be rated more highly than another who was a rising star for a short while and moved rapidly onwards and upwards? What allowance should be made for managers achieving results at a club with lower levels of resources even though this might appear – on the surface – to be a lower level of performance?

The chapter then goes on to discuss various factors which have been proposed as influences on football manager success. The impact of the level at which the manager played, experience and qualifications or context and issues such as finance are explored. The chapter also describes football managers in terms of their nationality and ethnicity – as these are both issues which are frequently discussed in relation to the future of football management.

Finally, the chapter concludes with some preliminary findings from research conducted by the author with co-researchers

Professor Larry Kahn of Cornell University in USA and Dr Amanda Goodall of Warwick Business School into the impacts of experience, expertise and quality of the squad on football manager success in different leagues.

What is success?

In management literature, "success" and "successful" are over-used words. Successful performance, successful leaders, successful results, but it is often hard to capture exactly what successful means. Is this in the short- or long-term? How will we measure this success? Should we only look at bottom-line performance? But then some companies who are growing fast do not make profits as this gets ploughed into growth. So perhaps success should include sales growth and market share, which might suggest financial benefit in the future. Or perhaps sustainable success will require building a good culture, encouraging innovation, hiring talented employees. If so, the achievement of these might count for success in itself.

Given that it is not always easy to see now what will bring results over the longer-term, management literature, therefore, struggles sometimes to identify characteristics in leaders and their organizations which will result in good performance. With the benefit of hindsight we can see which reigns were successful and less successful, but we do not always know whether this is attributable to the leader of the time or the building blocks put in place by their predecessors.

Many businesses are now increasingly results-driven. By this we may mean that there are accepted measures by which performance is judged. These are often specific to the particular industry, so we might be looking at the time it takes the NHS to see a patient or perform an operation, the exam results in a school or the number of academic publications in a university. In business we are often looking at some measure of sales, costs, profit and performance relative to the competition.

These measures result in league tables, rankings – often complex – which assess how well one hospital, school, university or business is doing compared to another. These are published and might provide the basis of decisions on funding, future business and even which organization prospective employees might wish to join.

Given the complexity of measuring performance in most fields, it is often with a certain relief that we look at a football league table where performance is measured in points for wins, draws or losses. Here is a business with clear-cut results and publicly accessible measures of success. Surely then we can look at the leaders of these football businesses, on and off the pitch, and decide first, whether or not they are successful and then, second, see what lessons we can learn about the experience, qualifications, technical ability or finances that are required to produce optimum success?

To an extent this is true. The following section looks at several ways in which we might measure success and what types of managers are successful using these different measures. It also looks at the influences of finance, level of experience, qualifications and other factors which might contribute to success.

At the same time, though, it soon becomes clear that even in football – the ultimate results business – success is not as simple as win, draw or loss. Therefore this chapter begins by considering how to measure the success of football managers.

What is success for a football manager?

Football is a results-driven business and its main "results" are wins and draws which give teams points in a league table. Regardless of what else is going on, whether the club is selling its squad, undergoing a phase of major rebuilding or turmoil, these results are published and are pored over by many millions of football fans globally. In this sense, success or failure as a football manager is clear cut and very public whether or not the collective failings of the club may have contributed to these results.

Yet, success as a football manager also has other facets. Gary Megson, until recently manager of Bolton Wanderers in the English Premier League, saw this at first hand. Whilst he kept Bolton comfortably in the Premier League in 2008–09 (finishing in 13th place out of 20) and reached the final 16 of the UEFA cup, the club's highest ever finish in European competition, he was booed by the Bolton fans in many matches. When asked why, fans responded that the style of play which delivered these results for Bolton was too defensive and was boring to watch. Fan pressure seems ultimately to have contributed to the departure of Gary Megson as Bolton boss.

On the other hand, West Bromwich Albion in 2008–09 were relegated from the English Premier League, although this was not a certainty until the last couple of matches. Whilst playing in the Premier League, West Brom were known for their attractive, attacking football. Several times they lost matches by the odd goal or were deemed unlucky. At the end of the season, West Brom manager Tony Mowbray was recruited to the position of manager at Celtic, one of the top two clubs in the Scottish Premier League and holders of a place in the European Champions League.

So which of these was most successful as a football manager? These examples suggest that we might measure individual success by:

- Results and the points which these bring.
- The track record of a manager at clubs and the extent to which he has progressed up the leagues. After all, West Brom's lack of points may well lie with the quality of their squad and not be a reflection on the ability of the manager.
- The results of the manager relative to the quality of their squad – has the manager achieved more or less than might have been expected given the players that they are working with?
- The style of play and the attractiveness of the football played by the club.

Additionally, other factors may constitute success. Dario Gradi at Crewe was known for development of a production line of youth players who came successfully through the ranks at Crewe both into their own team or were sold on at a profit to other clubs. Success for football managers, particularly in financially constrained clubs, might also then include:

- Developing youth players who can progress to the first team.
- Making a profit for the club by developing and selling on players.

This last type of financial success, might, however, detract from on-the-pitch success.

Measuring football manager success

The following discussion of what constitutes excellent performance for a football manager may seem to some pedantic! It is,
however, a simplification of the many discussions which I have
had with my co-researchers Professor Larry Kahn of Cornell
University and Dr Amanda Goodall of Warwick Business School,
about the success of football managers compared with the success
of various other types of business and education leaders.

The summary of how we arrived at our preferred measures of
performance in football managers are explained below.

The Castrol LMA football managers' performance table

First, let us draw the attention of anyone interested in the
performance of football managers to the excellent league table
produced by the League Managers Association. Based on
Prozone data, the Castrol LMA football managers' table is regularly updated and makes great strides in looking at the relative
performance of managers irrespective of the league in which
they manage (see Table 3.1). As the LMA explains: "The Castrol
LMA Managers' Performance table was devised to allow managers from every level of League football to test themselves against
one another."

The basis of calculation for the LMA Performance league is as
follows:

> Every competitive game counts towards a manager's individual
> score in the League. Points are awarded for victories and draws,
> with results away from home scoring higher. Points for clean
> sheets and goals-scored accumulate throughout the season,
> whilst a team's winning margin also counts towards the total.
> (http://www.leaguemanagers.com)

This data is produced into quarterly tables and is available from
2002 onwards. Once there is a sufficient history, this will clearly be
the performance measure of choice for any researcher and anyone
else who wants a comprehensive measure of success, as it balances

Table 3.1 The LMA managers' performance table as at 2 October 2009

1	Carlo Ancelotti
2	Arsène Wenger OBE
3	Sir Alex Ferguson CBE
4	Mark Hughes OBE
5	Simon Grayson
6	Phil Parkinson
7	Roberto Di Matteo
8	Rafael Benitez
9	Eddie Howe
10	David Moyes

Note: This table is for the 1st Quarter in season 2009–10 up to 25/09/2009.

the relative achievements of clean sheets, margins and home versus away matches in greater detail than any other single measure.

As our data and consideration of football manager success goes back to the formation of the Premier League in 1992–93, the data were simply not available for the time period and we went back to less comprehensive measures, as follows.

Win percentages and different kinds of success

If we want to compare managers by results over time, then a points total doesn't show how well one manager has done compared with another because they may have managed for different lengths of time, or show good cup runs.

Win percentage (and possibly also percentage of draws) is useful because we can use it to compare performances of managers irrespective of how long they were in charge, but it shouldn't be used without health warnings. For example, Table 3.2 shows a list of football managers who have all achieved a win ratio of 50 percent or more in managing English clubs since 1992. Immediately we begin to see some issues with the use of win percentages to measure performance.

Table 3.2 Football managers with win percentage over 50%, 1992 to date (as of 1 October 2009)

Manager	Club	Number of games	Number of wins	Win %
Arsene Wenger	Arsenal	745	428	57.45
Mark Robins	Barnsley	6	3	50
Kenny Dalglish	Blackburn	195	102	52.3
Eddie Howe	Bournemouth	35	21	60
Steve Coppell	Brentford (01/02)	54	27	50
Peter Taylor	Brighton	38	21	55.26
Mervyn Day	Carlisle	62	32	51.6
Gianluca Vialli	Chelsea	143	76	53.15
Claudio Ranieri	Chelsea	199	107	53.77
José Mourinho	Chelsea	185	124	67.03
Luis Felipe Scolari	Chelsea	36	20	56
Mark Wright	Chester (02/04)	120	63	52.5
Steve Bruce	Crystal Palace	18	11	61
Kevin Keegan	Fulham	61	38	62.3
Peter Taylor	Gillingham	62	34	54.84
Martin Allen	Leicester City	4	2	50
Roy Evans	Liverpool	244	123	50.41
Gerard Houllier	Liverpool	291	148	50.86
Rafael Benitez	Liverpool	304	175	57.57
Martin Allen	MK Dons	55	28	54.35
Paul Ince	MK Dons	33	55	60
Alex Ferguson	Manchester United	1286	754	58.63
Kevin Keegan	Newcastle United	251	138	54.98
Steve Coppell	Reading	122	62	50.82
Barry Fry	Southend United	30	15	50

(Continued)

Table 3.2 Continued

Manager	Club	Number of games	Number of wins	Win %
Steve Thompson	Southend United	14	8	57.14
Gudjon Thordarsson	Stoke City	154	77	50
Steve Bruce	Sunderland	9	6	66.00
Ossie Ardiles	WBA	55	30	54.55
Ray Matthias	Wigan	62	32	51.61
Gary Johnson	Yeovil	221	116	52.49

First, as a Sunderland fan I am delighted with the fantastic start that Steve Bruce had to his managerial reign at Sunderland. These data were taken up to October 2009. At this point some managers who were doing brilliantly, such as Steve Bruce and Mark Robins were early in their respective managerial tenures. When compared to other managers who have been in charge for longer, there are some who have done brilliantly for a season, or even several seasons, but overall performance tends to have ups and downs and overall performance may look less dramatic. This "central tendency" means that win percentages do not give due credit to managers for their excellent performances for a period of time during their overall tenure at a club (for example, Joe Kinnear's win percentage of 65.22 in 2001/02 or Peter Reid's 67.39 over the 1998–99 season). Moreover, it is clear that to keep a consistently high win percentage over a long period of time is extremely difficult.

Second, some managers achieve a high win percentage and are promoted on to higher league clubs. This "rising star" performance represents a different type of success to sustained success. If we split up the above table, then some of the managers have achieved excellent performance over a relatively short period of time (see Table 3.3).

Some of these managers are no longer at the respective clubs and, therefore, this is their "level of performance" which will always be recorded for their time as a manager at that club. Others, like Steve Bruce, Mark Robins and Eddie Howe are still at their clubs and

Table 3.3 Managers with high win percentage who managed under 100 games, 1992 to date

Manager	Club	Number of games	Number of wins	Win %
Steve Coppell	Brentford (01/02)	54	27	50
Peter Taylor	Brighton	38	21	55.26
Mervyn Day	Carlisle	62	32	51.6
Luis Felipe Scolari	Chelsea	36	20	56
Steve Bruce	Crystal Palace	18	11	61
Kevin Keegan	Fulham	61	38	62.3
Peter Taylor	Gillingham	62	34	54.84
Martin Allen	Leicester City	4	2	50
Martin Allen	MK Dons	55	28	54.35
Paul Ince	MK Dons	33	55	60
Barry Fry	Southend United	30	15	50
Steve Thompson	Southend United	14	8	57.14
Steve Bruce	Sunderland	9	6	66.00
Ossie Ardiles	WBA	55	30	54.55
Ray Matthias	Wigan	62	32	51.61

we are judging their success at a point in time. This performance may get better or worse as they have more games in charge – and is likely to go down over time. If we then take out those managers who are still in post, we have a list of managers who achieved very high success over a short period of time.

The other issue with total win percentage is that these figures include cup matches as well as league performances. As these may match lower league against higher league teams – and also in the current era may have some top teams playing their second string – it may be a fairer reflection on performance only to include league matches and to split down the data by season to highlight variations in performance over time. (See Table 3.4.)

Table 3.4 Highest win ratios over a season from 1992 to date

Year	Club	Manager	Win %
2004–05	Chelsea	José Mourinho	76.32
2005–06	Chelsea	José Mourinho	76.32
1999–00	Manchester Utd	Alex Ferguson	73.68
2006–07	Manchester Utd	Alex Ferguson	73.68
2007–08	Manchester Utd	Alex Ferguson	71.05
2001–02	Arsenal	Arsène Wenger	68.42
2003–04	Arsenal	Arsène Wenger	68.42
1998–99	Fulham	Kevin Keegan	67.39
2001–02	Manchester City	Kevin Keegan	67.39
2001–02	Plymouth	Paul Sturrock	67.39
1998–99	Sunderland	Peter Reid	67.39
2005–06	Reading	Steve Coppell	67.39
2002–03	Manchester Utd	Alex Ferguson	65.79
2005–06	Manchester Utd	Alex Ferguson	65.79
2004–05	Arsenal	Arsène Wenger	65.79
2005–06	Liverpool	Rafael Benitez	65.79
2000–01	Fulham	Jean Tigana	65.22
2001–02	Luton	Joe Kinnear	65.22
1993–94	Manchester Utd	Alex Ferguson	64.29
2007–08	Leeds	Dennis Wise	64.29
1994–95	Blackburn	Kenny Dalglish	64.29
1994–95	Carlisle	Mick Wadsworth	64.29
2000–01	Manchester Utd	Alex Ferguson	63.16
2001–02	Manchester Utd	Alex Ferguson	63.16
2007–08	Arsenal	Arsène Wenger	63.16
2003–04	Chelsea	Claudio Ranieri	63.16

(*Continued*)

Table 3.4 Continued

Year	Club	Manager	Win %
2001–02	Liverpool	Gerard Houllier	63.16
2006–07	Chelsea	José Mourinho	63.16
1995–96	Newcastle	Kevin Keegan	63.16
2002–03	Portsmouth	Harry Redknapp	63.04
1992–93	Newcastle	Kevin Keegan	63.04
2004–05	Sunderland	Mick McCarthy	63.04
2004–05	Luton	Mike Newell	63.04
2002–03	Wigan	Paul Jewell	63.04
1994–95	Manchester Utd	Alex Ferguson	61.90
1996–97	Bolton	Colin Todd	60.87
2008–09	Peterborough	Darren Ferguson	60.87
1997–98	Nottingham Fst	Dave Bassett	60.87
1999–00	Preston	David Moyes	60.87
2000–01	Brighton	Micky Adams	60.87
2003–04	Norwich	Nigel Worthington	60.87
1997–98	Manchester Utd	Alex Ferguson	60.53
2003–04	Manchester Utd	Alex Ferguson	60.53
1997–98	Arsenal	Arsène Wenger	60.53
2002–03	Arsenal	Arsène Wenger	60.53

An additional issue arises when we look at the clubs for whom the highest performing managers work. No one would wish to detract from the excellent achievements of the managers of the top four Premier League clubs who have demonstrated abilities, which have not only made them rise to the top of the tree, but in many cases have delivered consistently excellent performance. There are also eleven seasons in which Sir Alex Ferguson has achieved a win percentage over sixty percent, five in which Arsène Wenger has gained over sixty percent wins, three for José Mourinho and others for Rafael Benitez, Gerard Houllier and Claudio Ranieri. If we were to accept, though, that the depth of squad and quality of players in these clubs contributes to a level of success which is difficult to match for managers who do not have this level of resources, and to take out the managers of the Top Four for a moment, then there are perhaps clearer insights into into performance, as can be seen in Table 3.5.

Table 3.5 Highest win ratios over a season from 1992 to date (excluding managers of top four clubs)

Year	Club	Manager	Win %
1998–99	Fulham	Kevin Keegan	67.39
2001–02	Manchester City	Kevin Keegan	67.39
2001-02	Plymouth	Paul Sturrock	67.39
1998–99	Sunderland	Peter Reid	67.39
2005–06	Reading	Steve Coppell	67.39
2000–01	Fulham	Jean Tigana	65.22
2001–02	Luton	Joe Kinnear	65.22
2007–08	Leeds	Dennis Wise	64.29
1994–95	Blackburn	Kenny Dalglish	64.29
1994–95	Carlisle	Mick Wadsworth	64.29
1995–96	Newcastle	Kevin Keegan	63.16
2002–03	Portsmouth	Harry Redknapp	63.04
1992–93	Newcastle	Kevin Keegan	63.04
2004–05	Sunderland	Mick McCarthy	63.04
2004–05	Luton	Mike Newell	63.04
2002–03	Wigan	Paul Jewell	63.04
1996–97	Bolton	Colin Todd	60.87
2008–09	Peterborough	Darren Ferguson	60.87

(Continued)

Table 3.5 Continued

Year	Club	Manager	Win %
1997–98	Nottingham Forest	Dave Bassett	60.87
1999–00	Preston	David Moyes	60.87
2000–01	Brighton	Micky Adams	60.87
2003–04	Norwich	Nigel Worthington	60.87

First, it becomes apparent that many of the highest achieving managers are on this list because of a spectacular promotion-winning season. Second, that the same manager, having gained promotion might not achieve the same win percentage in the following season at the higher level. So whilst Peter Reid's management of Sunderland in the Championship in 1998–99 was excellent, his seventh place finish in the Premier League against much stronger opposition the following season does not make it into the list of highest win ratios. Which was the greater achievement? Likewise, Darren Ferguson's back-to-back promotions with Peterborough score highly, but his progress in the Championship, whether or not the club remains in the league, did not, even though he was pitting his wits against higher level opposition.

It should be noted that Martin O'Neill achieved a staggering win percentage of 75.5 percent over five years as Celtic manager. His comparatively modest 40.8 percent over three years as manager of Aston Villa might seem much lower but is an excellent performance given the challenges of achieving this level of performance in the Premier League given the relative levels of competition. This highlights the fact that financial status of clubs mean that some managers will never top these lists despite incredible achievements as managers: In this category are Dario Gradi, despite his monumental achievement in keeping Crewe in the Championship, or Sam Allardyce's achievements at Bolton and Alan Curbishley's at Charlton in keeping their respective clubs in the Premier League over so many seasons.

This would suggest that we need to mitigate performance against the level of resources that the managers have at their disposal.

So, whilst Luis Felipe Scolari's performance at Chelsea is impressive, he is judged relative to other managers at Chelsea and those other clubs who have comparable levels of resources at their disposal.

In sum, with a few notable exceptions, we get a better understanding of the success of football managers if we look at performance in terms of *win percentages* rather than points (possibly converted into average points per game), broken down *by season*, only including *league results* and balanced *against the quality of the squad available* to the manager.

The next section first reviews some of the potential influences on football manager success (see Figure 3.1) such as:

- Level at which manager played
- Experience
- Qualifications
- Finance and quality of the squad

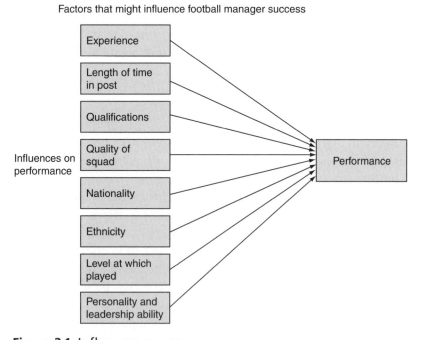

Figure 3.1 Influences on manager success

The level at which the manager played

How difficult is it to manage at lower level if you played at a higher level yourself? There are a number of examples of great players who were not great managers. Famously, Sir Bobby Charlton spent a brief period as manager of Preston North End, Maradona with the Argentinian national team, John Barnes at Tranmere.

In discussing why a great player does not necessarily make a great manager, commentators and analysts point to the intuitive nature of the talent of some excellent players, the individualistic nature of playing ability compared to skills needed to bring the best out of teams. There can even be a potential mismatch between the level at which the player played and that at which he has the opportunity to manage.

The above examples point to the fact that great players are very different to each other in terms both of individual characteristics and the teams they manage. The relative lack of success of these individuals as managers may have nothing at all to do with the level at which they played and much more to do with other aspects of management. After all, for every talented player who has not succeeded as a manager are others who have forged successful management careers.

Conversely, there are others, such as Arsène Wenger, Sven Goran Eriksson, José Mourinho and Gerard Houllier who did not play at a high level but became excellent managers. Does this suggest that individuals who were not great players make better managers; perhaps because they had to think more about how to play, that they learned how to develop skills themselves and can pass these on to others, or because they had other attributes that made them better able to bring out the best in others? Commentators point to Arsène Wenger as a great thinker and student of the game, Mourinho, the self-styled Special One for his charisma, Sven for his calmness and reflective ability under pressure and Fabio Capello for his discipline. Perhaps this suggests that there is no relationship between level played and success as a football manager and these instances of success or failure can be explained by other attributes?

Management research has looked at the question of whether expertise will make someone a better leader. Among leaders of universities, Goodall (2006, 2008) shows that the publication record of Deans makes them more successful leaders of research universities. In the sporting sector, Kahn (1993) looks at whether expertise in basketball makes good players better coaches. Expert leaders are also the focus of later work in basketball by Goodall, Kahn and Oswald (2008) which shows that the person's own level of attainment does influence their level of success as a coach. The typical basketball team finished six extra places up the league table compared with those coached by people who had not been great players. The authors consider several possible explanations for this.

- Perhaps this is the coach's acquired skill based on the in-depth knowledge of what wins matches.
- Perhaps they have played for and gained useful skills from great coaches.
- Perhaps some "tenacious personality" factor is at work. What made them a winner as a player makes them a winner as a coach.
- Maybe this is even something genetic that makes the person a winner.

In football terms, having been a great footballer might be expected to provide several types of expertise which could be useful to the manager.

- Great players might lead by example: "I have achieved this and you are also able to."
- This might relate to an ability to demonstrate a particular football skill, or to spot a potentially great player.
- It might mean that the manager has an understanding of how the game should be played at the highest level. "This is what we are aiming for."
- It could be that players at higher levels have networks among better clubs. Even if the manager is working at a lower level, they might be able to use their name and contacts to attract good players, or to get loans from the second string of higher level clubs.

- Perhaps the reputation of being a great player impresses the players of today.
- All of these might reasonably help the great players create a culture and help the manager to become a visionary and inspirational leader who players want to follow.

One explanation for why great players might find it difficult to manage players with lesser ability than themselves might be found in accounts such as that of Mark Lawrenson, who had spent much of his playing career at Liverpool, in his discussion of the brief spell spent managing Oxford United in 1988. Described by Liverpool FC's website as "one of the most elegant central defenders ever to grace the hallowed … turf" (http://www.liverpoolfc.tv/ news/drilldown/a_N164966090708-0801.shtml).

The reasons why the period as manager of Oxford United was brief are doubtless many and varied. Lawrenson himself highlights his sudden transition from playing to management:

> Once I snapped my Achilles, I always knew I was going to struggle to play again. I came back and played but it wasn't the same. After a while I said to Kenny that it wasn't improving and I went to see the specialists … So we went into his office and were told we had to stay for two days. He told me I would be carrying out a series of exercises over the two days and they would be filmed. At four o'clock the next day he told me to come into his office, and he asked me how I wanted the news. I said, "Just give it to me" and he said, "You've got to pack it in." I went back and told Kenny I was finished. That it was all over, and it was as sudden as that. Then, within a day, I was the Oxford United manager working with Maxwell, but that's a different story! (http://www.liverpoolfc.tv/news/drilldown/ a_N164966090708-0801.shtml)

Another issue appears to be that he found it difficult to coach players who could not do the things that he was used to players being able to do at Liverpool. At Liverpool you could tell a player to do something and they would be able to do so. This phenomenon also arises in discussions with other managers who have managed below the level at which they played:

> When I came in I wanted to give all the players the chance to show me what they could do. I wanted to be the type of manager who puts an arm round and encourages. The players seemed like they expected to be shouted at … but within weeks I found myself wanting to shout at them too. They just couldn't do the things that I was used to players being able to do. We would work on something in training, for example how to defend a corner and everyone would know who they were marking in that situation. The next match someone would not be marking their man and we would concede from a corner in the same silly way. It was very frustrating.

When asked about the benefits gained from being a well known player who went on to manage, one manager commented:

> The benefits of who I am lasted about six weeks. At first you get some credit from players because they know that you can do the things you are asking them to do, but that soon wears off. Then you're judged on whether you can manage and if you can't then your reputation won't be enough.

This might suggest that the combination of someone who played at higher level does not always work well with lower league players unless you have the ability to coach and manage as well as play well. One reason why higher level players might find the transition difficult is if there is a mismatch in expectations of the type of style of football which the players can play effectively. For this reason our analysis of successful football managers builds in a consideration of the level at which they played. Of course, defining a "great" player is in itself something on which we could write a book. For the sake of simplicity here, the players are classified into groups:

1 *Those who played internationally and in their top domestic league.* The requirement to have been both an international player **and** to have played in the top domestic league is decided

upon because some smaller international teams may take players who are the best of that nationality but are not playing at the highest level. So, for example, Wales, Northern Ireland and Scotland have international players who are playing in the second tier of the English game.

2 *Those who played in their top domestic league but not internationally.* These last group of international but not highest league players are also put into this category on the basis of their international caps, even if their league careers would not have put them into this group.

3 *Those who played in leagues below the top level in their country.* Any manager who played professionally but not in the highest league.

4 *Those who did not play professionally.* Whilst there are not many managers who fall into this category, there are still some. For example, José Mourinho is in this category, as was Stuart Murdoch at MK Dons and Lennie Lawrence at the various clubs he has managed.

The following section explores further the relationship between these two phenomena both in terms of the data and what can be learned from examples from press and other sources and from interviews with managers who have been in these situations.

So will Alan Shearer, Roy Keane, Paul Ince or Stuart Pearce necessarily be a better or worse manager because they were great players? Data first suggest that they are more likely to be appointed at the top level, perhaps because the fans want them to succeed, they will boost season ticket and merchandize sales or chairmen believe that they are more likely to command the respect of top level players.

In terms of their chances of success, as Roy Hodgson explained at a recent LMA event, "being a great horse doesn't necessarily make you a great jockey!" The skills of player and manager are very different. A great player may well have the aptitude to be a great manager, but may not necessarily. It can take time and experience to develop coaching and management skills. There is no substitute for experience and learning by doing. Sadly, in the turbulent world of football management, many young managers do not get long to get it right. The average tenure for a football manager currently stands at just under one-and-a-half years. Almost half of first-time managers never get another chance to manage.

There are, however, examples of managers who have managed to work across levels in this way. For example, Paul Ince at Macclesfield managed to turn around performance and keep the team in League 2. Martin O'Neill has managed across the spectrum of levels.

Conversely, there are many examples of managers who did not themselves play at a high level but have managed players of higher ability. One of the challenges here is for this type of manager to be afforded the opportunity to manage at this level. A majority of those who are examples of this ability gained their opportunity to manage outside of the UK. So Mourinho gained his first opportunity to manage in Portugal and had his first management experience with Benfica in the highest Portuguese league. Wenger, Houllier and Eriksson gained their first experiences in France and Sweden respectively.

Chapter 5 shows that the numbers of managers successfully progressing up the leagues is low. Relatively few managers who succeed at Championship level or below now get opportunities to manage in the Premier League other than if they are promoted into the league although the data show that, where they do get the opportunity, managers who did not play at a high level are able to manage successfully at this level.

Indeed, analysis of the relationship between individual playing experience and ability to manage suggests that these two interact differently depending on the level at which the player goes on to manage. For example, higher level players seem to perform particularly well as managers in lower league clubs (Bridgewater *et al.* 2010 forthcoming).

The role of finance

Gilmore (2000) sees the current era of commercialization of football as going back to the legacy of Berlusconi who established the link between clubs and TV rights in Italian football. When Berlusconi bought AC Milan in the 1980s, he bought rights to cover the club's matches via TV stations which were part of his portfolio of companies. The price paid for these rights raised the price paid by other bidders, such as RAI the state TV channel, for the rights to Italian live football. So decisions made in media and communications firms were closely tied up with success in Italian football in 1980s (Fynn and Guest 1994).

A similar commercial development occurred in the UK with the introduction of the Premier League in 1992 and the emergence of Sky as a broadcaster offering money for live rights. As BSkyB bid to get the rights to broadcast Premier League football matches live, other broadcasters needed to pay more to compete and the market for the TV rights to Premier League matches has continued to increase.

John Williams discusses the changing face of football in the 1990s. He comments on the cultural significance of sport, citing Jacques in *The Observer* who described the 1990s as "The Age of Sport." He highlights in particular the rise of sporting brands such as Nike and Manchester United which became the "commercial brands of the age" and also reflected on the shift in football ownership away from local businessmen to major City investors and media conglomerates who invest for reasons of finance rather than sentiment (Williams 1999). The nature of football investors seems recently to have shifted yet further as the trend for stock market flotation of football clubs has waned. The new breed of football investors are corporate institutions and billionaires from around the globe.

In 2008–09, nine Premier League clubs were under foreign ownership with Tottenham, Newcastle and Everton possibly set to increase those numbers, and FIFA President Sepp Blatter voiced his fears that the English game would become overloaded by debt and that the billionaires could walk away at any time (*The Independent*, October 2008). This fear is exacerbated by the current uncertain economic climate, which has resulted in possible financial difficulties for clubs whose investors have suffered financial reverses. The commercial development of football has dramatically changed the face of football management. Williams comments (1999) that:

> Managing a top club these days has become an extraordinary and skilful balancing act. The success of the Premier League itself

has added considerably to the burden. Judgment is everything here. To sign a top player for less than four or five years these days makes little sense; any shorter and one soon starts to wonder about losing his services to a rich predator for no reward ... Signing foreign players may raise questions about suitability and adaptability. At current wages a long contract for a top star could cost about £8 million – a costly mistake if things don't work out, especially if your prize asset becomes unwanted and perhaps unsellable, say within a year. (Williams 1999: 61).

It is clear, that like it or hate it, football has shifted from being "the beautiful game" to a game whose clubs are businesses. Some of these may be local businesses, but many operate on a global stage. Archie Norman commented at the recent LMA Management Conference at the Emirates Stadium that football is a business with a difference in that it is susceptible to investors who come in because they are rich fans rather than because the businesses are commercially viable (http://news.bbc.co.uk/1/hi/business/8278449.stm).

The impact of commercial development on football is in many ways positive; regeneration of football stadia, better safety and policing, bringing a fantastic game to a larger viewing audience through live television coverage, attracting the brightest talent into the English game. The changing face of football has brought with it unprecedented financial growth in recent years. Total finances in English football rose to almost £2.5 billion in 2007–08. The English Premier League grew by 26 percent to £1,932 million in revenue, an operating profit increase of around 95 percent up on the previous season. This revenue growth was largely fuelled by the new broadcasting deals from 2007/08 to 2009/10.

Broadcast revenue of Premier League makes up a significant proportion of the money that comes into the club. The new broadcasting deals were worth £2.7 billion over three years. Broadcast revenue in this league stands to increase, despite the demise of Setanta, given that there is scope for further development of the international market for live rights.

The average compound annual growth of the Premier League clubs from its formation in 1992 to date has been 16 percent.

It should be noted that this growth has been at its highest in the two years following the announcement of new broadcast deals. This was the case both in 2006/07, 2007/08 and similarly in 2000/01 and 2001/02. In both instances the revenue gained from the broadcast deals was spent almost in its entirety on player wages. In the recent period, 97 percent of the £351 million increase in broadcast revenue has been spent on player wages.

More worryingly, wage costs in the Championship also increased in 2007/08 by £32 million (12 percent) whilst the revenue growth has been more marginal. Revenue increased by 2 percent in 2007/08 but when parachute and solidarity payments are taken out of the equation there is a decline in revenue in the Championship. Even if we assume a revenue growth of 2 percent, the increase in wages over the last two seasons has been three times greater than the increase in revenue.

Some Championship clubs have spent more on wages than they have earned in revenue. In 2007/08 these clubs included Hull City (124 percent), Coventry City (121 percent), Southampton (116 percent) QPR (113 percent) and Burnley (110 percent). For some clubs, this is not a problem given that they have rich benefactors who are prepared to put money into the club. In the normal run of things, however, clubs who exceed their revenue face financial difficulties. These have been avoided by Hull City and Burnley, whose speculation on player wages resulted in promotion to the Premier League. High wage bills tend to be associated with clubs who are pushing for promotion.

Difficulties may also be faced in some instances by clubs who have been relegated from a league. In a BBC article, for example, Jonathan Rawcliffe reflects on the "slippery slope" which faces some clubs when they are relegated from the Premier League. Some of these clubs go onto to be relegated a second time from the Championship into League 1. This has been the case for 14 clubs since the formation of the Premier League. Clubs such as Charlton Athletic, Southampton and Norwich City have all recently faced this situation. Only one club, Manchester City have, thus far, rebounded from relegation into League 1 to the Premier League. A further five clubs, including Leicester, Barnsley, QPR, Sheffield Wednesday and Nottingham Forest have regained Championship status.

The reasons for this rapid decline may in part be psychological as confidence takes a blow when clubs are relegated (Paul Dickov commenting on Manchester City's relegation (http://news.bbc.co.uk/sport1/hi/football/8050784.stm).

They may also have a financial element. Whilst clubs may build into player contracts the ability to reduce player wages on relegation, few clubs have a further clause which covers the wage reduction which is required in season three when parachute payments from the Premier League cease. Two clubs who experienced financial difficulty once parachute payments had ended were Leicester and Southampton; Southampton went into administration and both clubs were relegated from the Championship into League 1. Deloitte & Touche (2009) comments that the combination of reduction in revenue and inflexible wages structures can be fatal for clubs whose parachute payments end.

Recent reports also point to the level of tax liability of football clubs. MacIntyre of the BBC suggests (BBC Website http://news.bbc.co.uk/1/hi/uk/7741859.stm 2008) that over £28 million of tax money owed by football clubs has already been written off by HM Revenue and Customs. Only £3.5 million of this amount – accumulated by clubs who went into administration owing tax – was recouped after 18 clubs went into administration. Lord Mawhinney, Chairman of the Football League, suggested that there may be a need to introduce regulations to prevent this from happening.

A further challenge which arises for football managers from club finances is that of the implications which commercial development has had for competitive balance. In their *State of the Game* report (2006), authors at Birkbeck College, University of London, point to the growing revenue inequality between the top five Premier League clubs and the rest of the league, between Premier League and Championship, between the Championship clubs with parachute payments and the rest of the league.

In football, the ability of any team in a league to beat any other team is what makes a match interesting. With increases in finance have come disparities in how this is spread between clubs. The "Big Four" in the Premier League had the highest absolute increase in revenue in 2007–08 (£33 million per club). The revenue of Premier League clubs – other than the Big Four – increased by £17 million. Relegated clubs – who are bolstered by the payment of "parachute payments" for two years – have an average revenue of £16 million. Indeed the parachute payment itself is higher than the average revenue of a Championship club (£11 million).

Overall the health of football relies on the fact that the outcome of matches cannot be known before they begin. If the same richer clubs always win, the relegated clubs are promoted again in the following season and clubs who are promoted go back down at the end of the first season, football will have killed the "golden goose" which sustains it as can be seen in Table 3.6.

At the current time, the competitiveness of the Championship means that clubs may take two or more years to regain promotion. Some clubs do yo yo between the divisions (Sunderland, West Ham and West Brom having been promoted and relegated more than once since 2002–03). If this competitiveness reduces, and an elite group of relegated clubs or those with parachute payments are promoted again the following season, then fan interest and attendance will be reduced.

Whether or not you like the commercial development of football, the "beautiful game" is not going to return to the almost amateur ethos which prevailed up until the 1980s and it should be remembered that the game in the 1970s and 1980s had a series of problems – such as dilapidated stadia and hooliganism – which

Table 3.6 Bouncing back

Season	2002–03	2003–04	2004–05	2005–06	2006–07	2007–08	2008–09 to date
How many of promoted clubs relegated	1 of 3	2 of 3	2 of 3	1 of 3	2 of 3	2 of 3	1 of 3

have been greatly improved by the money which has come into the game.

Nonetheless, Deloitte & Touche show a clear correlation between the quality of the players and the sporting performance of the club. This is particularly strong relationship in the Premier League although, after three seasons in which there seemed to be a strengthening relationship also in the Championship, by 2007–08 the connection between quality of their players and performance is less clear. The figures cannot be examined in detail for Leagues 1 and 2 levels, as too many clubs do not report their wage bills separately. For earlier seasons, however, when data were reported, there is still a relationship between the quality of the squad and performance, although this is less marked than in the Premier League.

Deloitte & Touche's comparison of quality of squad (average wage bill) and finishing league position of the club provides valuable insights into how much managers are over- or underachieving compared to the value of their squad and what might be expected of them if clubs finished according to the position suggested by their finances. Using wage data from club's accounts compared with the final finishing position in the league, the following analysis shows some of the managers who have achieved the best performance relative to the finances they had available.

Table 3.7 is calculated by looking at how many positions Premier League and Championship managers finished above the position that their finances would suggest. The top performers have consistently – and often across more than one or several clubs – shown the ability to outperform expectations. Note that some clubs do not report their wage data and therefore managers of these clubs are excluded from this analysis[1]. It should also be noted that this type of analysis works against managers of the top four clubs as it is hard to go up many places if you are consistently in the top four league positions.

The stronger relationship between average wages and performance in the Premier League, compared with the Championship, makes the performance of managers who have over-achieved what would be expected given the quality of their players in the Premier League particularly impressive. Honorable mentions go

Table 3.7 Biggest "over-achievers" in the Premier League and Championship from 2003–08

Manager	2003–04	2004–05	2005–06	2006–07	2007–08	Total places above expectation	Average places above
Tony Pulis	5	6	6	7	10	33	6.6
Steve McClaren	7	5	–	–	–	12	6.0
Sam Allardyce	10	10	6	9	–7	28	6.0
Brian Laws	–	–	–	8	3	11	5.5
Billy Davies	–	11	10	1	–1	21	5.3
Paul Jewell	7	8	7	–1	–	21	5.3
Bobby Williamson	–	5	5	–	–	10	5
Ian Holloway	6	6	–5	0	13	20	4.0
Neil Warnock	3	4	3	1	8	19	3.8
Paul Sturrock	4.5^2	–	–1	0	10	13.5	3.4
Dennis Wise	2	3	–	–	–	5	2.5
Steve Coppell	–1	0	5	9	–1	12	2.4
Mark Hughes	–	–5	5	2	4	6	1.5
Mick McCarthy	–1	3	0	2	1	5	1
Mark McGhee	6	1	–4	–	–	3	1
Dario Gradi	3	1	–1	–	–	3	1

to managers who out-performed expectation in a single season and are not included in the above table given the absence of some of the data. These include Gary Johnson (Bristol City), Simon Grayson (Blackpool), Paul Simpson (Preston), Owen Coyle (Burnley), Alan Irvine (Preston) and Nigel Adkins (Scunthorpe United).

Consideration of finances is complicated by:

- Different profiles of the different leagues in terms of the availability of financial data.
- The extent of the relationship between finance and performance.
- The need to judge relative to other teams competing at that level.

For this reason, one of the factors which should be used to compare data is the league in which the manager plays.

Experience

Age and experience often combine in discussion of football managers. "We need a good, young manager" or else "we need an older, more experienced manager who has been there and done it." Such descriptions of age and experience do not take into account the fact that some managers begin gaining their experience very early and could combine youth with experience. Perhaps because their careers end prematurely, or else because they take coaching qualifications and begin to gain coaching experience early – sometimes whilst still playing – we shouldn't forget that there are good, young and *experienced* football managers as well as their older counterparts.

When setting up the course for prospective football managers, some of those counted as "old hands" who had progressed beyond the stage of being invited on the initial course, included Lawrie Sanchez and Danny Wilson, both of whom had over five years of managerial experience by their early 40s although Brian Laws, who had begun managing in his early 30s and had eight years of experience came on the course.

Sometimes commentators refer to managers as "young" when they mean "new" "first-time" or "relatively inexperienced in managerial terms" and other times this is merely a perception which is not based on actual age or experience. "Young" Aidy Boothroyd may be permanently referred to as such in the press because he was when he began managing. This chapter looks at the impact on football managers of *experience,* having been there and done the football managers role, rather than age – although in most professions these two go hand-in-hand.

Doing the job of football manager for an extended period of time implies success. Almost half of all first-time football managers do not get another job after the first, a further 30 percent do not get re-employed after the second job and so on. (For further discussion of the rates of attrition in football management, see Chapter 5). This is a business in which only the fittest survive. As well as the need to perform consistently over an extended period of time, the successful football manager needs luck or judgment in working for clubs who will keep their nerve when results take a downturn. Those who do survive become more successful over time.

There is a significant difference between the number of years experience and the win percentage of managers. Comparison of the two shows that managers with:

- No previous experience (33.12 percent wins)
- Ten years or more experience (45.13 percent wins)

There is a positive correlation between experience and win percentage. More experienced managers have higher win percentages. In particular, analysis shows that football managers with higher levels of experience have better success rates in managing in the Premier League, perhaps because they are more used to handling the demands of "star" players. In reflecting on the value of experience and what makes managers successful, Harry Redknapp suggests that knowledge of the game and judgment of players – presumably gained from experience – are key attributes of the football manager (*Daily Mail*, January 2007). Similarly, Simon Jordan, Chairman of Crystal Palace is reported (*Metro*, 2 May 2008) as saying that you cannot buy the "experience of the league" which his manager, Neil Warnock possesses. This view is supported by former manager, Lawrie McMenemy, reflecting on the difficult task facing young managers who come into high profile Premier League jobs. At a point late last season, when both Alan Shearer at Newcastle United and Gareth Southgate, at Middlesbrough, were locked in relegation battles, McMenemy harked back to the experience that young managers used to gain in the lower leagues and the challenges of taking on a task – which would be difficult for anyone – in a first management position.

Likewise, on his reappointment at Crewe Alexandra for the third time after the sacking of Gudjon Thordason, Dario Gradi mused that he feels that he is a better manager now because of his earlier experience (http://news.bbc.co.uk/sport1/hi/football/teams/c/crewe_alexandra/8289236.stm).

This is unsurprising, given that time spent doing the job of football manager must provide invaluable insights, contacts and the ability to remain calm under pressure. Those managers who have not found a "recipe" for success quite simply do not manage for over ten years!

In talking about this "experience" players often refer to being managed by great managers, or of being captain and leader of the team. Indeed, in his comments on the appointment of Gareth Southgate at Middlesbrough, Chairman Steve Gibson listed a set of attributes of a successful manager which included man-management ability and judgment of players but also "experience" (BBC Website, 7 June 2006). This would seem to suggest that experience as a player is the same as that as a manager (http://news.bbc.co.uk/sport1/hi/football/teams/m/middlesbrough/5052126.stm), although, after Southgate's dismissal and the appointment of Gordon Strachan, the importance of Strachan's experience as a football manager was emphasized.

Whilst undoubtedly these experiences do help players to understand the potential challenges, it is hard to decide how many insights they provide into the realities of the role. The later discussion of the "transition" from player to manager in football management would suggest that there is little substitute for actually doing the football manager job, although the contacts and leadership experience of playing may help towards success in management. When fans argue in favor of appointment of a player, a local hero perhaps with excellent on-the-pitch leadership skills as captain, there is an assumption that these characters have a natural ability to manage. If the argument of Chapter 2 is accepted, then football management is so different to playing in the skills which it requires that it should be viewed as a separate profession. The question then is how do football managers get experience?

Experienced managers have learned lessons through time, perhaps through making and learning from mistakes. They are also the survivors, those who through natural ability and learning over time have a proven ability to do the job. At a recent LMA dinner, were a table of eminent managers who had each presided over 1,000 games as a manager. The "1000 club" includes, among others, Sir Alex Ferguson, Harry Redknapp, Jim Smith, Neil Warnock, Lennie Lawrence and Dario Gradi. The point was made that, if current trends continue and manager tenure declines further (half of first-time managers do not get a second chance and managers do not progress up the league structure), then in ten years' time there may not be one, let alone a table full, of managers eligible for the 1000 club.

It should be noted that we cannot conclude from the higher win percentage of experienced managers that it is experience alone which explains their better performance. Experienced managers are, by definition, successful managers and they have often progressed up the ranks to clubs which have excellent infrastructure and resources. All the same, experience should be considered as a factor in football management success. So Jim Smith, on the LMA website, muses that, whilst it may not be necessary for all managers to start right at the bottom of the leagues, there is still value in having a few years of coaching experience before being thrown into a management role (LMA Website http://www.leaguemanagers.co.uk/news/news-99.html)

Qualifications

UEFA dictates that, to manage in the Premier League – with the possibility of admission into European football tournaments – a manager must possess the UEFA Pro Licence. This rule has been the subject of considerable debate. Sometimes clubs see this as a bureaucratic requirement and wish to appoint someone who has not yet reached this stage of their coaching "badges" or else has become successful without having gone through the process of gaining qualifications.

Among the more experienced managers, some argue that coaching qualifications have been useful:

> I know some people used to moan about taking time out of their schedule to attend courses, but I used to think if I get one useful thing, if I come away with one thing that I might do differently that would give me an extra inch, then it was worth it.

Whilst others, as in any field, suggest that experience is more valuable, maintaining that the badge in itself is less important than other attributes such as ability to spot a good player.

This debate, which might equally be happening in sales, IT or another function where the most successful managers do not always have the highest levels of professional or academic qualifications, sheds light on the different roles which qualifications can play. Qualifications provide evidence of a certain level of achievement and – hopefully – also provide useful insights, learning and skills in reaching this standard of achievement. Sometimes this can be used to work out whether someone who does not yet have experience has the potential to succeed in a particular role. Qualifications are not intended to replace experience but ideally to sit alongside experience such that a manager can benefit both from theory and practice.

In football, both as a response to a UEFA mandate that coaches in the Premier League should hold the UEFA Pro Licence (the highest level of UEFA's coaching and management "badges"), and to help to create a cadre of properly prepared and skilled coaches and managers, qualifications have become part of pathways into football coaching and management.

In explaining the need to professionalize football management, then CEO of the League Managers Association, John Barnwell, explained that managers used to learn from the experience of managing in lower leagues, often in conjunction with coaching badges such as the FA Full Badge. As fewer managers now progress up the leagues, some Chairmen appoint big name players straight into big management jobs which also come with high profile and big responsibility. Without the space to learn by trial and error, qualifications help to fast track and, whilst never a substitute for experience, help to prepare prospective managers for the challenges they will face. They will improve the chances of managers. In management education, qualifications are often split into pre- and post-experience. Students might study management at undergraduate and then Masters level immediately after undergraduate courses. These students do not yet have management roles but have gained the knowledge that will provide them both with a toolkit of techniques, problem solving and other skills as well as the ability to reason and present and support arguments. This will help them, should they choose, to go on to be Chief Executive Officers, Accountants and Creative Directors of the future.

Post-experience students may already have been on the career path towards these goals. For these students, learning can be compared with, and applied to, experiences to reflect and learn how best to manage.

Football management education might fulfil either of these roles, depending on when it is gained. Prospective football managers gain a toolkit which will help them to understand the nature of the challenge, hit the ground running and have the techniques and skills to tackle difficult situations. It might also provide insights to experienced managers who reflect back on situations which they have faced and work on better ways of handling these. It is not the intention that qualifications replace experience.

As Aidy Boothroyd explained:

> The idea is to take best practice from business and other sports to make sure that you can do things like deal with the media, manage projects, organise finances, read a balance sheet and so on. These make you more prepared. When you go into a Board meeting and people are talking about cash flow etc it's easier to understand now because you've had that training. It can never fully prepare you for that nasty question when you've lost a game but it goes a long way in helping to.

At the same time, the need to create a cadre of well prepared potential managers has long been recognized. How else should we address the questions that arise everytime the manager of a leading club or international team is brought in from another country? Why are home grown managers not being developed? Speaking when attending the PFA and LMA Football Manager Certificate at Warwick Business School, Stuart Pearce said:

> The course doesn't plan to send you out into the wide world as an accountant or anything like that but it gives you a feel for what is going on away from the football side of clubs. To me the bottom line is the more education you can give yourself, and the more preparation you can do, the less chance of failing. That's my philosophy. (Stuart Pearce, England 21 Manager, Warwick Business School 2004)

If the routes to achieving success through experience alone are becoming more difficult – if not impossible – then surely there is an argument to make every effort to help young managers to succeed. Ideally, qualifications in football would sit alongside experience of coaching and managing. When they do so, the manager has additional insights and is able to put these into practice. Mark Hughes, whilst manager of Blackburn Rovers reflected that he has heard another manager saying that he did not realise the state that his club's finances were in but had thought to himself that he would have done because he had looked at the balance sheet as an example whilst on the PFA and LMA Certificate course at Warwick Business School (*The Sunday Times*, 13 October 2002).

In addition, as in other fields, qualifications do provide evidence that a coach or manager has reached a certain level:

> For someone like myself, who played only lower league football and at the moment only coaches and manages within the same environment, qualifications are the only way to prove that you have the capabilities to work at a higher level. (Sean O'Driscoll, Manager, Doncaster Rovers FC, www.wbs.ac.uk)

Moreover, proponents of lifelong learning believe that it is never too late to learn a new skill or ability or to hone those that already exist. The skills might become less vocational as an individual has reached the top of their career tree (and they might even learn a musical instrument, a foreign language or something outside of professional life). For middle managers, however, the need to move from being a specialist to a generalist, or to learn new abilities to progress often prompts a return to learning.

Given the debates put forward in the last two sections, perhaps the ideal combination to help a football manager to become successful is experience and qualifications, rather than either one or the other on its own.

Nationality

There are frequent discussions about the difficulties which young British managers face in making it to the highest levels of football management. As many of the top clubs are foreign-owned and have star players drawn from around the world, they also draw from a global pool of football management talent.

In fact, the trend towards having foreign football managers is perhaps not surprising, if we step back and look at the international development of football as a game. In international business literature in the 1960s, Perlmutter (see Figure 3.2) described the development of multinational corporations as a "tortuous evolution" in which companies evolved through stages from "ethnocentricity" in which international operations were directed from a home country base and a majority of staff were from the home base, through to geocentric – corporations such as Unilever, Nestlé or Philips being good examples – where the organization is so global that it is hard even to detect the original nationality and employees and management may be from many countries and continents.

Figure 3.2 Perlmutter's evolution of the multinational firm 1966
Source: Harvard Business Review (1996).

In some ways, the commercial development of football has brought with it an internationalization of the resources which go into clubs. Even at lower levels, squads are made up of many different nationalities. In the Premier League it is not now uncommon to field a first team line-up which has no home grown players. Ownership is increasingly international, with some clubs owned by investors from a range of countries and continents. One such example is that of Arsenal, which currently has ownership split between UK, USA and Russia.

Given the global audience for football, it would be easy to assume that football clubs are now "geocentric" organizations, much in the style of a Nestlé or Philips. There are, however, a number of fundamental differences:

- The game has a global audience although often each country also has an audience for its own clubs and league.
- Where there is a global audience for a national game – such as for English Premier League football – this takes the form of an export with rights negotiation happening from the home country. Television broadcast rights are sold and distributed in different markets, but the game is hosted and played in the home country.
- Football has some global (e.g. World Cup), some regional (European or Asian Champions League) and some national competitions. Whilst some clubs compete at a regional level, most, other than the top clubs in the Premier league compete nationally. Those clubs who compete regularly in Europe, and the clubs within Europe who aspire to do so, are most likely to employ a foreign manager.

It is, however, to be expected that there would be a gradual increase of foreign managers even within clubs who operate at a national level, because international players, with good experience of the English game, may be seen as options who could use networks of contacts in particular markets, might be linked with a style of play which seems attractive to the club's owners and indeed might come from the same country and culture as the owners.

There is no expectation that managers of different nationalities would be better or worse than each other. Nationality is, however, analyzed to show what trends have taken place in football management, not least because of the perennial debate about developing prospective English England managers.

Within the Premier League,[3] Table 3.8 shows the split of managers by nationality 2008–09. And Table 3.9 shows the nationalities thus far for the 2009–10 season.

Whilst the Premier League has had international managers such as Scolari from Brazil and Avram Grant from Israel, they are still in a minority compared with managers from the EU and UK. The total number and percentage of managers from England, UK and other regions since the formation of the Premiership in 1992–93 is shown in Table 3.10.

In its first season, the only Premiership manager from outside the UK was Joe Kinnear (Republic of Ireland). Five others; Ferguson, Graham, Dalglish, Souness and Porterfield (half season), were Scottish and the remainder were English. The nationality of managers in the Premiership is now diverse, as would be expected given the global profile both of the league and the English game.

Table 3.8 Mix of nationalities of managers in Premier League in 2008–09

English	Other UK	Non UK
Steve Bruce	Alex Ferguson	Joe Kinnear
Tony Mowbray	Martin O'Neill	Arsène Wenger
Roy Hodgson	David Moyes	Rafael Benitez
Gary Megson	Tony Pulis	Luis Felipe Scolari/ Guus Hiddinck
Harry Redknapp	Mark Hughes	
Sam Allardyce		
Gareth Southgate		
Tony Adams/Paul Hart		
Kevin Keegan/Alan Shearer		
Phil Brown		

Table 3.9 Mix of nationalities of managers in Premier League, 2009–10 (as at October 2009)

English	Other UK	EU
Steve Bruce	Alex Ferguson (Scotland)	Gianfranco Zola (Italy)
Phil Brown	Martin O'Neill (N Ireland)	Roberto Martinez (Spain)
Gary Megson	David Moyes (Scotland)	Arsene Wenger (France)
Mick McCarthy	Mark Hughes (Wales)	Rafael Benitez (Spain)
Paul Hart	Tony Pulis (Wales)	Carlo Ancelotti (Italy)
Harry Redknapp	Alex McLeish (Scotland)	
Roy Hodson	Owen Coyle (Scotland)	
Sam Allardyce		

In the last five years, around three-quarters of managers have been from the UK, around half of these being English. There are currently eight English managers in the Premiership, the same as last year. At the current time, the five managers from outside the UK are all from the EU.

Table 3.10 Mix of nationalities of managers in Premier League in its first season (1992–93) compared with 2008–09

Nationality	92–93[4]	03–04	04–05	05–06	06–07	07–08	08–09
English	16.5	11	8	10	11	8	8
Other UK	4.5	4.5	6.5	5	5	5	7
Total UK	21	15.5	14.5	15	16	13	15
Non-UK	1	4.5	5.5	5	4	6	5

Football management, it would appear, has moved over time from the ethnocentric to the regional stage of international development. There is little evidence that it has moved into the polycentric stage – given that Scolari and Grant, both ex-managers of Chelsea, are the only managers from outside of Europe. Other than this, football management has shown some international development as would be expected given the global development of the game and its investors, but still reflects the acknowledged expertise of home-grown UK football managers.

Ethnicity

PFA statistics suggest that in excess of 20 percent of football players are black whilst only three of 92 (3.26 percent) of football league managers are black. More broadly, black football coaches also account for only a small proportion of the total population of football coaches. A quick look through club websites reveals only a few; Chris Ramsey (Tottenham), Steve Brown (Wycombe), Terry Connor (Wolverhampton Wanderers), Andrew Cole (Huddersfield) and Les Ferdinand (Tottenham).

The imbalance between the proportion of black football managers and coaches compared with that of black players suggests an issue worthy of further research. Whilst considerable progress has been made in eradicating racism from football's terraces, is this a new glass ceiling which must be broken through? Research conducted in 2004 on behalf of the Football Association showed that all of those interviewed would feel happier if the number of black coaches and managers (and indeed football administrators) stood at a level more in keeping with Britain's multicultural society.

Much has been written recently on the issue of black coaches and managers, in the press, by the football bodies and by others with an interest in diversity. The following section draws on the findings of the author's 2004 research for the Football Association which was carried out with the assistance of the Professional Footballers Association and League Managers Association. It is based on interviews with black coaches and managers and football management statistics. Where appropriate these have been supplemented by other secondary interview material to determine whether the views expressed reflect broader concerns.

The disparity between the proportion of black players and black managers suggests that the question of why there are not more black football managers and coaches merits exploration to identify inhibitors and facilitators in the process of creating a football coaching and management community which more nearly resembles that of football on the pitch.

Commentators, such as Garth Crooks, point out that the disparity between the representation of black players and black coaches and managers might even amount to exclusion of a section of society from coaching and management (BBC Sport 22 February 2007). Others, such as Ralph Rodgers, Walsall Physiotherapist suggest that the gap between the two numbers is so great that it seems unlikely that it is a statistical anomaly (BBC WM Documentary 2007; also Simon Austin BBC Website 2007 and Matt Slater BBC Website 2009). As the reasons for the gap are queried repeatedly, most respondents felt that there was a question worth answering. Indeed, in general, black players, coaches and managers interviewed for this research perceived themselves as having a lesser chance of success than their white counterparts. They worry that this could have a racial explanation although few know for sure. This section attempts to synthesize the debate on why there are not more black managers and explores the factors that may hinder the progress of black players to management as well as those that the respondents feel help.

The statistics

There have been 30 appointments of black managers in all leagues since the 1992–93 season. These involved 17 different managers. Keith Curle and Keith Alexander have each held three posts, Paul Ince and Leroy Rosenior four – if the latter's brief return to Torquay is counted – Chris Kamara, Carlton Palmer and Ruud Gullit have each held two posts during this time period. John Barnes has held one English post – although had previous managerial experience at Celtic and with the Jamaican national team. Two of the black Premier League managers, Gullit and Tigana came from outside of the UK. The only black English

Premier League manager who came up through the management ranks in England has been Paul Ince, whose tenure at Blackburn was less then six months.

As we are dealing with a small number of managers, it is difficult to draw significant statistical inferences. Accordingly this section presents only descriptive statistics and offers tentative comparisons between black managers and the total population of football managers since 1992. (See Tables 3.11 and 3.12.)

Table 3.11 Black managers 1992–93 to date

Name	Club	Appointed	Left
Viv Anderson	Barnsley	01-Jun-93	02-Jun-94
Chris Kamara	Bradford C	27-Nov-95	06-Jan-98
Ruud Gullit	Chelsea	10-May-96	12-Feb-98
Chris Kamara	Stoke	22-Jan-98	08-Apr-98
Ruud Gullit	Newcastle	27-Aug-98	28-Aug-99
Andy Preece	Bury	30-Dec-99	06-Dec-03
Noel Blake	Exeter	10-Jan-00	24-Sep-01
Leroy Rosenior	Bristol City	14-Jan-00	27-06-00
Jean Tigana	Fulham	01-Jul-00	17-Apr-03
Gary Bennett	Darlington	02-Aug-00	24-Oct-01
Ricky Hill	Luton	10-Jul-00	15-Nov-00
Carlton Palmer	Stockport	06-Nov-01	18-Sep-03
Garry Thompson	Bristol R	24-Dec-01	09-Apr-02
Leroy Rosenior	Torquay	09-May-02	19-Feb-06
Keith Alexander	Lincoln C	05-May-02	09-Apr-06
Keith Curle	Mansfield	04-Dec-02	11-Nov-04
Carlton Palmer	Mansfield	20-Dec-04	19-Sep-05
Keith Curle	Chester	29-Apr-05	19-Feb-06
Iffy Onuora	Swindon	30-Sep-05	22-May-06
Leroy Rosenior	Brentford	14-Jun-06	18-Nov-06

(Continued)

Table 3.11 Continued

Name	Club	Appointed	Left
Keith Alexander	Peterborough	30-May-06	15-Jan-07
Paul Ince	Macclesfield	23-Oct-2006	25-Jun-07
Paul Ince	MK Dons	25-Jun-07	21-Jun-08
Paul Ince	Blackburn	21-Jun-08	16-Dec-08
Paul Ince	MK Dons	06-Jul-09	To date
Keith Curle	Torquay	08-Feb-07	17-Feb-07
Leroy Rosenior	Torquay	17-May-07	17-May-07
Keith Alexander	Macclesfield	27-Feb-08	To date
Chris Hughton	Newcastle	27-Oct-09	To date
John Barnes	Tranmere	14-Jun-09	09-10-09

Table 3.12 Black managers by league

League	Number of Managers
Premiership	4
Championship	4[5]
League 1	10
League 2	12
Total	**30**

The proportion of black managers remains low – around 3 percent of all managers appointed since 1992–93 have been black – particularly in relation to the proportion of black players (PFA numbers suggest that in 2003 more than 20 percent of players were black).

The number of black manager appointments has increased since 1999–2000 with a peak in 2001–02 when five of 92 football manager jobs went to black candidates (see Table 3.13). The number of black managers in post peaked in 2001–03 when six of 92 (6.52 percent of managers) were black. Four black managers

Table 3.13 Black football management appointments by year 1992–93 to date

Season	Number of black managers appointed	Number of black managers in post	Managers in post for all or part of season
92–93	0	0	
93–94	1	1	Anderson
94–95	0	0	
95–96	2	2	Kamara, Gullit
96–97	0	2	Kamara, Gullit
97–98	0	2	Kamara, Gullit
98–99	2	1	Gullit
99–00	3	3	Gullit, Preece, Rosenior
00–01	2	5	Preece, Hill, Blake, Tigana, Bennett
01–02	5	6	Preece, Blake, Tigana, Palmer, Thompson, Bennett
02–03	0	6	Preece, Tigana, Palmer, Rosenior, Alexander, Curle
03–04	2	5	Preece, Palmer, Rosenior, Alexander, Curle
04–05	1	4	Palmer, Rosenior, Alexander, Curle
05–06	1	5	Palmer, Rosenior, Alexander, Curle, Onuora
06–07	4	4	Rosenior, Alexander, Ince, Curle
07–08	2	2	Ince, Rosenior
08–09	2	2	Ince, Alexander
09–10	3	4	Ince, Hughton, Barnes, Alexander
	30		

Note: year end is taken as 31/05 of each season.

were appointed in 2006–07 but only two were in post at the end of the season. A further two, Paul Ince at MK Dons and Keith Alexander at Macclesfield, were appointed in 2007–08 and these two remained in post at the year end (31 May 2008). 2008–09 saw the appointment of Paul Ince back to MK Dons and John Barnes at Tranmere. Four black managers have been in post at some point this season. Chris Hughton overlapped John Barnes only in a caretaker capacity so a maximum of three at any time.

Whilst a significant number of black managers are first-time managers, and not all progress to further managerial appointments, it should be noted that these figures are not out of line with the attrition rates among the total population of football managers. Forty-nine percent of first time football managers are never appointed to a further management post. Of those who get a second post, a further 28 percent are not appointed a third time (see Table 3.14).

For the black manager sample, ten (58.8 percent) managed once and seven, a second, third or fourth time (41.2 percent) as shown in Table 3.15). However, if John Barnes is actually a third

Table 3.14 Management exits in total population of managers

Times managed	Number of managers	Number not appointed again	Percentage exits to appointees
One	276	138	49.07%
Two	137	39	28.47%
Three	99	38	37.36%
Four	61	21	34.43%
Five	40	13	32.5%
Six	27	13	48.15%
Seven	14	7	50%
Eight	7	6	85.71%
Nine	1	0	
Ten	1	0	

Table 3.15 Number of times managed to date

	Number of Managers
First-time managers	10^6
Second-time managers	3^7
Third-time managers	2
Fourth-time managers	2

time manager then this shifts to nine who were reappointed (52.9 percent) rather than with eight (47.1 percent) and of course this is a snapshot in time so Chris Hughton, or other first-time managers may go on to gain additional posts.

In order to gain additional insights, this report moves beyond the statistics to data drawn from in-depth interviews with black players, coaches and managers. These are presented as a set of barriers and facilitators of the recruitment of black football managers.

What stops black managers from being recruited?

Institutional racism?

There is agreement that massive progress has been made in tackling racism in the English football game. Paul Ince comments in the Evening Standard (Paul Ince, *Evening Standard*, 6 February 2007) that the levels of racism in football are much better than they were in the 1970s and 1980s and that this should be attributed to the work of the FA, Kick it Out and other anti-racism movements.

Yet there is a general feeling that the treatment of black and white candidates for football management is not equal. Some respondents seem clear that there are racial overtones and others are worried that there might be, but were not sure:

Do the numbers. It just doesn't stack up. Everyone has been told that this Chairman or that Chairman would never appoint a black manager, but there is never any evidence.

I would hate to think that I don't get jobs because of the colour of my skin. You put in your CV and pray that, if you don't get it, that's not the reason why. It might just be chance, it might be that there are so many good candidates, but it does sometimes go through your mind, what if …?

In attempting to explain why such a small proportion of black players become managers, interviewees and media reports often provide cases that are ascribed to racism. Until his recent appointments with Jamaica and at Tranmere Rovers, John Barnes was the most commonly cited instance of a black manager who only had one opportunity to manage. This lack of reappointment was often put down to racism (Oliver Holt, *Daily Mirror,* 31 January 2007):

> Why has John Barnes not ever got another football management job when he was such a good player? Surely he merits another chance?

This linking of ethnicity with opportunity was also seen in other instances with questions such as:

> Why was Paul Ince passed over in favor of Mick McCarthy at Wolverhampton in summer 2006?
> Why did Paul Ince begin his management career at Macclesfield, at the bottom of the league whilst Roy Keane and Gareth Southgate began much further up the leagues?

The Holt article (Oliver Holt, *Daily Mirror,* 31 January 2007) which refers to the gap in John Barnes football management career between Celtic and Tranmere also pointed to the fact that, at the time of the article in 2007 and indeed now, there are no black managers in the Premiership. At that point there was also no black manager in the Championship, although Chris Hughton at Newcastle in March 2010 sits top of the Championship table with Newcastle United. It is perhaps easy to draw comparisons, as he does, between the path into management of Paul Ince and Roy Keane, both great players, and attribute any differences to ethnicity.

These are unproven and dangerous assumptions. Whilst we cannot know for sure that race did not play a role and, if this is the case it is incumbent upon us all to ensure that an equal opportunities policy is followed, there are many other plausible explanations. Niall

Quinn is a younger Chairman and had played alongside Roy Keane; Mick McCarthy had direct experience of getting a club promoted from the Championship to the Premiership on a limited budget and had the requisite UEFA Pro Licence should Wolverhampton be promoted in 2006–07. Almost half of all first time managers go out of the game and are never re-appointed. Several candidates who have come through coaching and management qualifications had great playing careers but do not walk straight into football management jobs, a majority of these are white candidates. It may well be that the reasons are more complex than ethnicity and probably relate to the over-supply of prospective managers to jobs not to mention the number of experienced candidates who also struggle to get further management jobs.

As can be seen earlier in this chapter, there are a number of plausible explanations for why a football manager might succeed or fail and for what type of manager is appointed. Let us be clear that racism in any form is to be deplored, but it is not possible to be clear whether or not there is a clear relationship between ethnicity and success of appointment. The following are among many alternative explanations for these decisions:

- Level of experience
- Level of experience in particular league
- Qualifications
- Club structure
- Club context
- Nature and background of Chairman
- Relationship between Chairman and prospective manager
- Average tenure of first-time managers
- Proportion of first-time managers who are not reappointed.

To allay the perception that the recruitment process is not fair, clubs should be encouraged to adopt a transparent and professional recruitment process.

The recruitment process for football managers

There has long been a discussion about club's and managers appointing their pals to positions. This can lead to problems – sometimes these people may not be the best candidates for the job, they might be too similar to the people appointing them – rather than bringing complementary skills – and the result is a game where who you know becomes more important than what you know. Whilst this is changing slowly, and football posts are often advertised through specialist recruiters, the field of candidates is still narrower than in many sectors. This might be wholly appropriate to save having to filter out large number of fan applications for posts for which they do not have the professional background, but it may bias football posts towards social networks rather than drawing candidates more broadly from the the professional game.

Frustration with the process of transition from playing to management emerges from many conversations with ex-players and prospective managers regardless of ethnicity. It is also a dominant theme in discussions with black players, coaches and ex-managers:

> There are a percentage who battle through the system and keep looking and keep trying but there are a majority who just see that the paths aren't great and assume that they're going to struggle. There are other paths where they see black people succeeding, like in the football media and as pundits and they think "I could do that as well/better than some of them ..." but they are looking at the lack of black managers and thinking they don't stand much chance. We are talking about percentages. A percentage will look and think maybe there isn't much chance.

The recruitment process appears to be becoming more professional. Many league clubs invite applications, produce a shortlist based on CVs and interview once or maybe twice. The interviews of selected candidates may last up to a day and some involve external recruitment specialists. There is consensus that this should happen as in most walks of life:

> People should be allowed to be interviewed and properly assessed, based on their record and CV.

This is still not, however, always the case. Instances are cited of staff recruited without qualifications or prior experience, of preferred candidates appearing and being fast-tracked though a selection process, even of there being no selection process outside one preferred candidate.

If the recruitment process was clear and transparent, all concerned would have greater confidence that it is fair and likely to produce the best candidate regardless of who or what they are. As Paul Ince puts it in the *Evening Standard* (6 February 2007) it shouldn't matter what color you are, black, pink, green, so long as you can do the job well.

Broader societal trends

> Going back in time society saw black people as different. In areas of power and authority, in football that would be Chairmen etc they would accept black players but they didn't see them as management material. The system did have prejudices but they were hidden. That wasn't just the case in football. In all areas people looked at the black guys and thought well they may be good workers but they aren't management material. They took the view that black people weren't efficient enough to be governing. It takes time to release those prejudices.

The link between the lack of black football managers and a broader lack of black managers in other professions emerged from conversation a number of times. There was a perception that black people are not viewed as being effective in managerial roles. This is seen as something which is changing:

> Over the years it has happened. We have a more multicultural society. There is far more contact with black people and they are taking on management roles. As it has changed, the ideas and prejudices have diluted. There still aren't many black faces in boardrooms. Not as many as you would expect there to be. In football I don't see many – or any? – black faces in boardrooms.

Similarly, Paul Ince refers to the possible prejudice of Chairmen against black managers as "a generational thing."

What can help black managers to be recruited?

Where does the process begin?

> It goes back to the system. Most of the coaches will have been players first and they start creating ambitions and plans for the future early on. If they can see a path and know that there are opportunities they will be more inclined to follow a path through.
>
> This does go back into the roots of the system. We need to encourage black participation all the way back into the Academies and with players, not just with coaches and at the stage of managerial appointments. Leaders on the pitch often become the managers of the future – sometimes though player-coach or player-manager roles as a transition to management. Sometimes also the future managers are those handed responsibility by their managers of the time. These are transferable skills. If the captain shows fire and brimstone, it may mark them out as a future manager. (See Figure 3.3.)

Will it get better over time?

Some of the transition along the arrow shown in Figure 3.3 – and eventually into football management – is felt to be happening over time:

> I think there is a time dimension to this. This is about the transition between playing and coaching. At one time it was about the acceptance of black football players. At the moment there are plenty of black players and they are now more accepted but there are plenty of high profile players who have finished

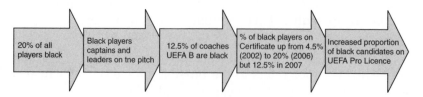

Figure 3.3 Stages of encouraging/identifying black managers

and not enough of them have made it through into coaching and management. There is a frustration because some people thought it was just a generation thing. As those players finished they would progress but as time have gone by it seems that it isn't that simple. That has caused a frustration – black players haven't seen a path through. There are lots of coaching courses. At first the black players weren't attending those in sufficient numbers but now when you go on the coaching courses there are enough attending. They are showing the desire and about the right proportion of black players/black coaches are there. Maybe it could still be a bit higher.

There are issues. At one time there were very few black coaches on the courses but I see a larger proportion there now. I think some of this is a generational issue. The early black players clearly faced horrific racism and were the pioneers who raised awareness of the issues and made things better for the players who came after them.

The role of coaching/football management qualifications

Some black players, coaches and managers feel that attending courses is about "ticking boxes":

> It is important that black coaches take away all the excuses. How can anyone tell if there is institutional racism? Chairmen are not going to tell anyone that this is why someone is or is not appointed. But if there is no excuse, it is harder to turn down a good black candidate.

Others question the motivation to go through coaching qualifications, without the incentive of football management jobs at the end of the process:

> It is a lot of work to get your badges, to get all the qualifications. If you think "Is it worth going through all of this" – and I am sure there are black coaches who have thought this – "Will I have to go abroad to get a job or perhaps not get a job", then I can see why some black players might not bother.

Table 3.16 Black candidates with UEFA
Pro Licence or FA Coaching Diploma

Name	Year Completed
Noel Blake	2002
Chris Hughton	2002
Hope Powell	2003
Chris Ramsey	2006
Paul Davis	2006
Leroy Rosenior	2007
Ifem Onuora	2007
Keith Alexander	2007
Andy Preece	2003 Diploma

Table 3.16 lists the black candidates who have completed the English FA's UEFA Pro Licence or hold the FA Coaching Diploma.

Whilst the participation of black candidates on coaching courses is much higher than it was, one or two candidates suggested that the criteria for the FA's UEFA Pro Licence and the PFA/LMA Certificate course could be an issue. Both require a UEFA A licence and give priority to candidates with first-team coaching experience. If black candidates struggle to gain coaching positions within clubs, then this could also affect their ability to get onto the courses that might help them to progress.

Another interviewee reflected on an instance, which he high-lighted as something which could have been interpreted as racist – although he made it clear that he believed this was probably not the case:

> I was invited on a fast-track UEFA B course but injured my hamstring and couldn't run so was unable to attend. The fol-lowing year I didn't receive an invite, but I heard that there had been an issue about no black candidates being on the list and shortly after received an invite. I was interested, applied, came to the FA and completed the paperwork. The course did

not run, I think it was because of a lack of numbers and I was never invited again."

The interviewee later started working through coaching badges, but heard that a white candidate, of comparable playing ability at a different top club was doing his badges within that club rather than on a general course with candidates who had not been professional players:

"I'm not saying its racism but you can see why someone might interpret it that way. You can see why someone might look at it and say the white guy is getting better treatment – why? I was as good a player.

A clear and transparent process for how and why some candidates appear to be treated differently to others might help to allay this type of concern.

Should there be positive intervention?

In the USA, NFL has adopted a voluntary rule known as the "Rooney Rule" which says that two minority candidates should be interviewed for any football management or front office vacancy. There are fines for those who do not comply with the rule.

In the UK there is no such positive discrimination legislation and this may be difficult to introduce as clubs have more autonomy from the league's governing body than in the USA. Recent reports have debated the potential merits of some form of positive discrimination in "giving the process of increasing the number of black managers a shove."

Positive role models

A high percentage of players now see the route into coaching by doing their badges. When they come to sit in front of directors and boards of football clubs – they are being judged for what they would be like as managers. There is a frustration because they think they won't stand a chance. The black players haven't seen enough black people going through and succeeding. Often they think – well he is a bigger name than I am and if he can't succeed then what chance am I going to stand and they don't bother.

The lack of positive black role models for young black players and coaches was identified as an issue by Brendon Batson (BBC 22 Feb 2007 Sport) although this seems likely to change as black English players, like Paul Ince and Chris Hughton, come through the system and succeed, rather than successful black managers coming in from abroad. Future generations of black players may be more inclined to believe that they can succeed as football managers. These players do not need to be big names, although big names attract attention and may have a bigger impact in the early stages of their football management career.

Ralph Rodgers, a black American working as club physiotherapist at Walsall is clear as to the benefit of high-profile black players becoming managers. Moreover he believes that it is right that these high-profile individuals highlight the need for a debate on the current lack of black football managers. He applauds Paul Ince for speaking up on the issue in 2007, likening him to black champions such as Mohammed Ali and Jesse Owens who spoke out against any possibility of racism in order to move forwards. Another manager thinks it is about success stories as well as about high profile players:

> We need a black Aidy Boothroyd, someone who comes through the system, does the badges, is appointed and does really well. That might start to change perceptions among the next generation of black players.

The structure of football clubs

Another suggestion is that changing football club structures might help to change the proportion of black football managers in England. International investors might, it is hoped, be more prepared to recruit diverse candidates on merit who are not necessarily in their own image. Some think that the change towards more foreign ownership may result in a more diverse set of football managers in England. When you consider that there is not a single black chairman or director at any of the 92 league clubs, the suspicion that the off-the-pitch profile of football has some bearing on the preferred candidates in football management in not surprising.

It is not clear that this will expectation of greater diversity will necessarily be the case. Racism can exist equally in many cultures and one bias might well be swapped for another, but – in theory – greater diversity of ownership might result in greater diversity among football managers.

Persistence and preparation

> It is possible to view race as half-full or half-empty. It might be something that you have to overcome but that can drive you on and make you more likely to succeed. It is important to break down the barriers but this is an active thing rather than about passively waiting for something to change in the system. Black players need to get themselves onto the courses, they need to badger for jobs. I have received very positive feedback from other managers around the system because of how hard I work and how positive I am.

This view was one which recurred throughout meetings with black players, coaches and managers. Whilst some felt that they had missed out on opportunities, a majority were more keen to talk about what could be done to move forward – what could be done to change the situation.

Initiatives such as the PFA's Black Coaches forum were welcomed. Here help is given by circulating information about jobs, advice, help with CVs, encouraging candidates onto coaching courses. Earl Barrett, a player who became involved in the Black Coaches forum commended it for the encouragement it offered and for the positive role models of black players succeeding as coaches and managers. He went on to work through his UEFA coaching badges and is now coaching in Stoke City's Academy.

Perceived success: viewing success through a lens

In addition to the challenges which the lack of competitive balance within and between leagues poses for football managers, the position of the football manager is also complicated by the scrutiny of several stakeholders:

Fans

Fans have exacting – and sometimes unrealistic – expectations of what the manager can achieve. Whilst some managers will over-achieve relative to expected performance, this is still little protection against fans and even boards who may have unrealistic expectations of what is possible given the quality of players available.

Data collected from Premier League fans in 2001 gave insights into how success as a football manager breeds ever increasing expectations among fans. Whilst Ipswich Town – who had been promoted under George Burley into the Premier League – were sitting fifth in their first season and were ranked as exceeding expectations by their fans Manchester United, who won the Premier League were still rated by their fans as under–achieving. They were not as successful in Europe that season as in earlier seasons and had won the treble three seasons before. It is clear that success, even when measured by results, is not an absolute but something in which previous performance and indeed the history of the club will play a role. So, for example, if a team has previously played at a higher level and their fortunes and finances are currently at a lower point, it is difficult for the fans to appreciate that the gaps between leagues may make it difficult to get back to where they came from.

Media

As discussed in Chapter 2, the intense media spotlight on managers intensifies the pressures under which they work. The advent of Sky television with its multiple camera angles and the ability to view and review every gesture, grimace and celebration of football managers has combined with the insatiable thirst for material of the 24/7 sports news channels and the internet to create a new level of scrutiny for football managers.

As early as October 2009, newspapers were already speculating about who would be the first Premier League football manager to be sacked. Seven games into the 2009–10 season, Paul Hart, manager of Portsmouth was forced to comment that he had nothing to fear (*Daily Mail,* 25 September 2009) in the face of reports linking Gordon Strachan, David O'Leary and others to his job (*Sunday People,* 27 September 2009). A similar story was being played out at Hull City with papers declaring that Phil Brown had only six weeks in which to save his job at Hull City (24 September 2009).

A Google search reveals 609 articles speculating about the future of Paul Hart and 288 regarding Phil Brown. Bookies even invite punters to lay odds on the football "Sack Race" as though the football managers, as much as the game, are part of a sporting contest. In his recent book, Barney Ronay (2009) comments:

> The modern football manager adorns not just the front and back pages but the middle ones too … The job itself has changed fundamentally. Being a manager is now a kind of televised public performance. With his windmilling arms and spittle-flecking displays of emotion, the modern football manager is a magnetic figure. He reminds us of a stadium evangelist or a charismatic young leader of the opposition. Strutting and telegenic, his gestures are thrillingly decisive, his utterances destined for interminable reinterpretation. (Ronay 2009: 1)

Whilst this all adds to the spectacle and excitement of football for fans and media, it may well be that the speculation about a manager's future might influence the decisions made by the Board of the club. If they perceive the manager to be very unpopular and if they worry that this may rebound onto the Board itself if they are not seen to take decisive action, then this attention may lead to the manager being dismissed. At the very least, media attention might amplify the impact of good or bad results for a football manager.

Football managers and success: the big picture

This section is based on analysis carried out by Professor Larry Kahn, Cornell University, for joint research with the author and Dr Amanda Goodall of Warwick Business School. Full details of this research can be found in Bridgewater, Kahn and Goodall (2010 forthcoming).

As expected, teams at the higher level have higher levels of resources – better players – to work with. In real terms, the wage bills at the highest level have been almost 19 times those which managers in the lowest league have to work with. We might also guess that those who played at a higher level themselves are more likely to be managing at that level and this proves to be the case. Over time a greater proportion of great players have been recruited at the top level. Across all of the seasons since 1992, almost half of the managers in the Premier League have themselves been international players – and a further 36 percent played in the top league domestically.

Compare this with League 2 – the fourth level of English football – and there have only been 18 percent of managers who played internationally (so for example managers like Paul Ince who managed Macclesfield) and a further 19 percent who played in their domestic highest league (for example Martin Allen, who until recently managed Cheltenham in League 2 but played himself for West Ham). The managers at the top level are also more experienced than their lower league equivalents. They have over 9.5 years of experience on average, whereas in League 2 the average length of experience has been 3.6 years (see Table 3.17).

Table 3.17 Playing history of football managers since 1992

	League			
	Premier League	Championship	League 1	League 2
Manager played internationally	0.500	0.362	0.270	0.181
Manager played top domestic league	0.091	0.172	0.191	0.199
Manager played in other leagues	0.354	0.386	0.443	0.508
Manager never played	0.056	0.078	0.091	0.110
Manager's average experience (years)	9.629	6.494	4.807	3.619

We split up the managers into the leagues in which they managed, and measured their performance by the position they managed in their respective leagues. We then looked at the following questions:

- *Does the quality of your squad make a difference to performance?*
  As discussed in the previous section (page 82), Deloitte & Touche show a relationship between the quality of players and sporting performance for the Premier League and a relationship – although less marked – in the Championship and the impact of player quality seems to be reducing in the Championship in recent years. We also include data for other leagues (most clubs reported this data until around 2001–02) and discover that the relationship between how good players are and success works here too, though less strongly than for the Premier League.
- *Do better players make better managers?*
  It seems that better players succeed more than those who were less good as players particularly in lower leagues. Maybe the players at lower levels are more inspired by the example of these players, or perhaps – when they become managers – the better players can use their network to bring in a better class of players into the clubs which they manage.
- *Do you need experience as a manager or will playing experience substitute for this?*
  In higher leagues, the effect of experience appears significant. Managing star players in the full glare of the media spotlight is not easy and it may be for this reason that managers who have been there and seen it before are better able to manage at this level.

Overall we conclude that:

- There is an interplay between experience, the level at which someone played and the level at which they manage as well as with the value of the squad so that particular combinations of factors seem to influence success. We see, for example, that being a great player has a larger effect at some levels than others. Similarly, experience matter more in the Premier League than for managers in lower leagues. Money matters, particularly in the Premier League. Likewise, improving the quality of the squad does improve sporting performance. It does not appear that moving up the rank order of clubs spending big on player wages brings a place for place improvement in performance, but it does tend to result in a higher placed finish.

- According to our estimates, in the year 2000 if you moved a club from the 75th to the 25th centile rank in wages (a move equivalent to increasing your budget from the 15th to 5th highest in the league) you would go up about six places in the league. In other words, increasing spend on players improves performance but probably not in proportion to the level of spend.

- If you step up the spend on players in a club managed by a top player you may gain an average five places in the league but this increases to an average eight or nine places if the club is managed by a manager who was not a great player himself. In other words, managers who were not great players themselves are better able to manage good players than worse.

- How good a player the manager was seems to have a bigger impact when they manage lower down the league structure. The improvement in performance gained by top players seems to be greater with these players than with players who are also great.

- More experienced managers seem better able to manage at the highest level. We can speculate why this might be. Perhaps experience helps them to cope with the foibles of star players. Perhaps they are better at coaching these players or determining tactics – regardless of how good they were as players themselves. Of course, it may simply be that the managers who survive long enough to gain long experience are the survivors who had better ability through force of personality, charisma or playing reputation to manage star players. This effect is only seen at Premier League level suggesting that there is something distinctive about managing these strong egos and that management experience does help with this.

- The complex interplay between these different abilities suggests, however, that expertise in playing the game and expertise at football management are different and distinct abilities. One cannot be assumed to lead necessarily to the other.

Conclusion

Whilst football might seem to be a clear results business, it is still important to consider how success should be measured. There are various possible measures, from points and league tables to win percentages over different periods of time. The actual level of success may also be different to the level of success perceived by fans, media or Boards of Directors. So a club which is actually performing well might still not be delivering at the level expected by its various stakeholders. This tends to result in unfortunate consequences for the football manager.

By using different measures of success – straight forward win percentages, those which divide managers up by length of time managed and so on – we arrive at different sets of managers who might be considered most successful. If we then mitigate our assessment of success by taking into account the level of budget – and hence quality of players – available to the manager, we might get yet another list of those who have achieved well relative to what they have available.

To determine who is doing well – and to make sensible judgments as a business about resource deployment, continuation of employment and so on – it is important to use the most accurate data possible on performance and to use whatever method in the knowledge of any shortcomings it may have. It would seem important that perceived success should be recognized as a distortion of actual success.

There is still potential for further work to gain better insights into what contributes to success by further discussion of the different influences in conjunction with each other – rather than separately – and this will allow for optimal decisions by football clubs about who to employ and when it is time to move on.

CHAPTER 4

The Blame Game: Does Changing Leaders Help?

We were awful at times but United gave Sir Alex that vital ingredient: time... We seem to be wrapped up in getting instant success now. Would another manager, even at United, get the time that Alex was given to get things right? I'd like to think so, but I'm not sure. "But he got it right and people like me, who played for him, haven't got a hope of copying what he's done. He's incredible." Speaking ahead of the visit to Old Trafford, [Steve Bruce] added: "Even in the tough times when I first went there, he was driven, he was a winner. He made all of us who played for him better." (www.football. co.uk/manchesterunited)

Introduction

When a football club's performance dips, the fans point the finger first at the manager and players. If the manager is then sacked and the club wins a match, the reaction is that of vindication "see I knew it was the formation, playing one upfront, playing that player on the left, the manager had obviously lost the dressing room." As a manager is most commonly dismissed after a poor run of results, the Board may also feel relieved that they have been seen to take decisive action and that this has turned fortunes. But is sacrificing the manager the right decision?

On 26 October 2009, Barnsley played Manchester United in the fourth round of the Carling Cup competition. Regardless of the result, some parts of the the press coverage in the run up and the aftermath of the match were clear already. Attention focussed on the two managers, Mark Robins recently appointed manager of Championship club Barnsley and Sir Alex Ferguson, manager of Manchester United. Headlines pointed to Mark Robins as another excellent young manager who played under Sir Alex Ferguson – Steve Bruce, Mark Hughes, Paul Ince, Bryan Robson have already gone into management, as has Sir Alex's son Darren Ferguson. More particularly though, they revisited the vital goal scored by the young Mark Robins against 7th January 1990 when he played for Manchester United. The team were going through a blip at the time and there were calls in some quarters to get rid of Sir Alex and install another manager. Mark Robins is popularly reputed to have saved Sir Alex's job and the rest, as they say, is history.

As we now look back at Sir Alex's record of success at Manchester United, at his eight Premier League titles, five FA cups, the treble in 1999, one of only three football managers (alongside Brian Clough and Bob Paisley) to win the European Cup three times, it seems incredible that anyone could ever have doubted his ability to manage Manchester United successfully. Yet if newspaper accounts from the time are to be believed, a more trigger happy Board could have done just that:

> January 7, 1990, a pivotal day in the career of Sir Alex Ferguson. Skipping through the football annals now and seeing the bare statistics of United's 1–0 win at Nottingham Forest in the third round of the FA Cup, thanks to a Mark Robins goal, might seem to the casual observer a meaningless statistic. Yet it will be remembered by supporters of United and others with long footballing memories as the day the course of history was changed and Ferguson launched himself and his club upwards on a power curve that shows no sign of taking a downward trajectory. Yet it all could have been so different. Manchester United might not have gone on to dominate the game almost to the point of boredom and Ferguson might not be regarded by his peers as the Godfather of their profession if Forest manager Brian Clough had been victorious that day. ("Remember When … Defeat Could Have Meant the Sack for Sir Alex at Man Utd", Ian Edwards, www.footballfanhouse.co.uk, 5 August 2009.)

So if a decision could have been so wrong, how many other sacked managers needed only the turn of fortune, which inevitably comes at some stage? How many other managers could have gone on to long and distinguished careers at a club from which they were sacked?

Moreover, when the manager **is** changed, what are the consequences – positive or negative – for the club? The club may get an immediate and sustained upturn in results and be sure that this was the right decision. Or they may get a short-term upturn and no discernible longer term benefit, or even a worse performance as a result of the change.

Whatever the effect on results, the club will have to pay compensation for some, or all, of the manager's remaining contract, fees to lawyers to reach a settlement, possible compensation to another club if they want to appoint a manager who is already in a job. The new manager might not like the players at the club and so there will be fees to agents and possibly the need for a transfer budget. This is all money which goes out of the club when they change manager. Some clubs may even change manager more than once a season. From the outside it seems like madness, particularly if the club is already cash strapped.

From the club's – and fans' – perspective each switch is approached with optimism and every victory under a new manager greeted as evidence that this is money well spent (even though the Board and fans may be the very people who greeted the last manager with similar optimism) a short time ago.

This chapter begins with a discussion of what we can learn about the impacts of changing managers and succession from management theory and goes on to explore what is likely to happen if an organization changes managers regularly. Football management experiences extreme levels of turbulence and is a good vehicle to look at the implications of managerial succession for the performance of organizations.

Football manager succession

In the broader field of management, conventional wisdom also suggests that changing leaders will improve organizational performance. The time horizon for a new Chief Executive isn't long enough for a new vision to be fully implemented – or, much as with a football manager, the fruits may ripen some time after the manager who planted the seed is gone, and the next incumbent may be credited with the success of a predecessor's actions.

There are two schools of thought on whether changing leader helps performance. In favor of change are studies such as those of Hofer (1980), Schendel *et al.* (1976) and Bibeault (1982):

> a precondition for almost all successful turnarounds is the replacement of the current top management ... Usually ... the old management has such as strong set of beliefs about how to run the business ... many of which must be wrong for the current problems to have arisen, that the only way to get a new view of the situation is to bring in new top management. (Hofer 1980: 25–6)

This view is supported by Schendel *et al.* (1976) who argue that to gain a recovery after a period of decline requires "explicit action by management." Similarly Bibeault (1982) argues that in 70 percent of the changes of manager, top executives are replaced either:

> because (1) They cannot cope with the problem effectively or (2) because they are themselves the problem.

In three quarters of the turnarounds, the turnaround attempt is headed by people who are new to the job because:

> to succeed, a turnaround must begin by destroying [the] atmosphere of hopelessness and discarding the world view that led to it. Since both are embodied in the organization's people, especially its top management, the top management as a group must be replaced.

In the football context, this argument raises a number of important questions – and raises conflicting views on what it is best to do if performance has taken a downturn.

1　What is the problem?
2　Does it require this radical a solution?
3　Who are the top management?
4　How many of these would need to be replaced to change
the "atmosphere of hopelessness" (to borrow Bibeault's
terminology).

What is the problem?

In some ways it is understandable that football organizations look
at a decline in performance and decide that changing management
is the way of achieving a turnaround. The problem in a football
club is – usually – that the team is losing matches, or else failing
to make sufficient progress towards some kind of stated goal.

*What is considered an insufficient level of performance
is not absolute*

Luton Town had lost only three of thirteen matches and lay just
outside of the play-off positions in 2009–10 but had not found life
as easy as they expected in the Blue Square Premier league when
they parted company with their manager. In the same season,
Northampton Town had lost four of eight matches before changing
their manager. The trigger points for managerial change differ club
to club. It is not uncommon that a manager could be sacked for a
performance which is acceptable at another club.

What constitutes acceptable performance is perhaps judged in
relation to resource availability – how else could Mourinho be
sacked as manager of Chelsea for lying second in the Premier
League? Performance is not actual, but is judged in relation to the
expectations of the Board and the fans (See Chapter 3 for further
discussion of this issue.)

Is it a downturn or a blip?

When management literature talks about the need to change
leadership because there is a need for turnaround, it is not clear
that many football management situations fall into this category. Few football managers last long enough to preside over a

Table 4.1 Time of year when managers dismissed 1992–93 to date

Season	Jul	Aug	Sept	Oct	Nov	Dec	Jan	Feb	Mar	Apr	May	Jun	Total
92–93		0	2	2	1	1	3	4	1	3	5	3	31
93–94	6	2	3	4	3	5	4	1	3	1	2	3	31
94–95	0	3	6	1	8	4	3	3	5	9	4	6	52
95–96	0	0	2	5	3	4	5	4	2	2	4	1	33
96–97	1	5	4	3	6	3	3	5	2	1	8	3	45
97–98	2	2	2	3	4	3	2	4	5	3	8	6	44
98–99	2	3	4	3	4	1	1	0	2	3	7	4	36
99–00	4	3	2	4	4	3	3	4	4	2	5	3	38
00–01	1	5	4	5	4	4	4	6	5	1	3	2	45
01–02	3	2	6	13	2	4	4	3	4	8	4	4	56
02–03	2	1	1	7	1	1	2	2	5	4	5	2	31
03–04	0	2	5	3	3	3	3	4	7	3	4	5	42
04–05	0	4	1	4	8	4	4	1	2	2	6	2	39
05–06	1	0	5	1	2	3	3	6	2	3	14	5	45
06–07	2	0	5	4	4	6	3	2	4	3	5	2	40
07–08	0	0	3	8	4	2	2	4	1	1	5	1	31
08–09	0	0	4	2	5	6	4	4	1	4	2	1	33
09–10	1	2	3	6									12

sustained period of decline. If they do, it is because the decline is attributable to causes which are clearly not under the control of the football manager.

Dismissal of football managers rises sharply in October and November – the season having begun in August. Two months into the season, it is clear which managers have got off to a good, or disappointing, start to the season. The data presented in Table 4.1 show the pattern of football manager sackings by month.

When are football managers dismissed?

Overall, the pattern of manager dismissals shows two peaks. There is a peak in May/June, at the end of the season, and a second peak in October/November. The pattern was examined over time to see if it has changed. The peak in October/November did not exist in the earlier years (only 1992–93 is shown for clarity) but emerges clearly in recent seasons. The October/November peak was at its highest in 2001–02, and may be a result of the introduction of the transfer window. This second peak fell back from 2002–03 although it reappeared in 2007–08 and sometimes happens rather later in November and December.

The difference between a win, draw or loss might, however, be down to as narrow a margin as which side of the post a rebounding ball falls, whether a penalty is awarded or denied, a sloppy goal conceded in injury time. These quirks of fate are not the engrained "hopelessness" which Bibeault (1982) talks about as requiring a change of leader.

There are a number of reasons why football clubs might be inclined to act at this point. Some are structural. If the transfer window opens in January, why give transfer money to a manager in whom the board no longer has confidence? That money might better, they argue, be given to a new manager to help build a different team.

Whether performance would have changed without a change of management is the basis for endless speculation. The case of Sir Alex Ferguson clearly shows that the poor run ended by Mark Robins' goal was just that – a blip in a stellar management career. For many others who were sacked at that point, we will never know if the luck would have turned, particularly if performance is judged very early in the season. Management theory suggests, however that performance does go through ups and downs and usually rebounds without intervention.

Why are performances poor?

One of the major differences between the management literature on CEOs and the situation of football managers lies in the question of how much influence the football manager has on the decisions that are made and the atmosphere surrounding the club. In sacking the manager, the inference is that these things lie at the football manager's door. Yet the context surrounding the dismissal may well be that the club is in a broader period of transition. Perhaps the club has suffered a downturn in finances – falling gates, end of parachute payments, cancellation of matches for poor weather, loss of an investor, previous financial problems and resulting point deductions resulting in relegation. If the reason for the downturn in performance is not attributable to the football manager, but comes from broader contextual problems in the club, then changing the manager, or even the manager and all his staff, will not solve the problem.

A change is as good as a rest?

In some sectors, there is an inbuilt cycle of changing leader. Prime Ministers and Presidents face periodic elections and are reappointed if they have delivered, are popular, or are at least better than the other candidates. In creative industries, there is sometimes a belief that the leader has a preferred style and that creativity will be greater for changing leader every now and again. In European football clubs, the head coach may be replaced every couple of years. There would appear almost to be an expectation that this will happen. Continuity at the club does not lie with the head coach, however, but is retained by keeping the same Sporting Director.

Is this cyclical change a benefit to the English style of football management? Changing the manager in this case might mean changing the whole structure of the football side of the club; manager, backroom staff and ultimately players. Two months into the 2009–10 season, Steve Bruce, at Sunderland, had already sold two players back to Roy Keane at his new club Ipswich, several others to Stoke City and had already declared an intent to release more players from the previous regime who are surplus to requirements now that his new signings are in place. Change on this scale is both an expensive and disruptive process. Given the possibilities that the new team may take time to gel, this is not necessarily a quick fix.

New manager is allowed more scope to make changes

When considering why a new manager might achieve better results, authors point to the fact that the new manager is often given more latitude by the board of directors than the previous incumbent. This results in organizational and strategic level change (Greiner and Bhambri 1989). A new manager might perform better because the conditions under which he operates are different. Perhaps the players who were injured are coming back into the side? More likely the new manager uses the greater bargaining power which he has on appointment to negotiate a transfer budget which could not be secured by the last manager. Maybe the Board sees this as a fresh start and has a greater confidence in his ability to sign "great" players who will take the club forward.

Why was the manager changed?

Rotherham had begun the 2009–10 season strongly when manager Mark Robins moved on to Championship club Barnsley. When the change of management happens not because of dismissal or poor performance – whether actual or compared with expectations – then the challenge for the replacement manager is different. Here is a team which is working well and a new manager must step into the role without affecting the team's performance.

Does it require this radical a solution?

A number of reasons for poor performances are temporary. So, for example, a downturn might be made up of a run of poor results in which the team performance has actually been quite good, or good in parts. There could have been injury problems which will get better over time. The sequence of fixtures might involve playing all the top teams and other periods might have a more favorable run of fixtures in which the manager would expect a better haul of points. On the other hand, the reasons for the poor performance might go back to the quality of the players, the recent sale of the best players, the transition between one team and a new team. It is not uncommon for managers to get their team in place during pre-season or even after the season has started and for them also to work with a far greater number of short-term loans than might previously have been the case (See Chapter 1 for a fuller discussion of the challenges of football management). In this case, the downturn might not be something which is likely to be changed by bringing in a new manager and might only be addressed by more radical measures – a boost in revenue, new investment, the move to a new stadium.

Who are the top management?

In management research, the top team who provide strategic leadership are the Board of Directors led by the Chief Executive Officer. Hofer (1980) makes a distinction between operational and strategic levels of an organization, noting that real turnaround usually involves the strategic level of the organization and cannot be addressed by operational changes.

The football side of a club may be run entirely by a football manager – who identifies, negotiates, trains and develops players and determines the line-up and tactics for particular matches. Whilst this might count as "strategic" management – and is certainly critical for success of the team – this day-to-day running of the organization might still be counted as operational. So training sessions and organizing players to play effectively might be operational, depending on how much control the football manager really exercises in the club. In this case, changing the football manager is only an operational switch. This being so, prevailing wisdom from management theory suggests that changing manager is unlikely to result in a major turnaround in performance.

How many staff would need to be changed?

Building on the above discussion, it is not clear whether more radical changes in personnel – such as new ownership – would be needed to really change the fortunes of a football club. In some instances, even changing owners might not make a major impact because underlying problems such as the size of the support or the ownership of the stadium might be barriers to major change. The current league position of the club might also mean that changing fortunes will be a long-term project. A fascinating case study is that of Notts County, who have changed ownership and set their sights on a rapid rise up the league structure. As this book year to press, it would appear that this is not an easy or quick process.

On the other hand, changing the football manager without the rest of the staff might not result in any major changes in the culture and processes in the club unless a new manager can make sweeping changes. Depending on their finances and beliefs, clubs vary in whether they might leave backroom staff in place or allow a new manager to bring in his own staff. Theory would suggest that the extent of the change made when a manager leaves also determines how big an effect this has on longer-term performance.

The blame game

Studies of how effective it is to change leader also talk about the role of "scapegoating" where the change of leader is done for symbolic reasons. From the Salem Witch trials to foreign policy, having a "bad guy" can be useful for organizations who are performing badly:

> The dismissal of a chief executive officer can be interpreted as a public display of the underlying power structure of the firm. Witness the recent American Express, IBM, Westinghouse, and General Motors announcements concerning decisions made about executive succession in those firms. Rumors about who is in and who is out reign supreme under such conditions. (Mainiero 1994)

"Scapegoating" originated in biblical times. The term refers to the process of addressing community sins which were confessed and symbolically placed on the head of a goat that was sent into the wilderness. More recently scapegoating has come to mean "avoiding responsibility for wrong doing by blaming someone else" (Gibson 2005). Sociologists, political scientists and organizational theorists who try to understand the reasons for, and the impact of, top management dismissals are interested in what these cases reveal about the power structures within organizations. They are more interested in dismissals, than those cases where the leader changes because of retirement or voluntary departure (Fredrickson, Hambrick and Baumrin 1988). In the case of dismissal, research has shown very different effects. Opinion differs and dismissing a manager might result in disruption, better performance or no difference in performance. The answer to which of these will happen seems to lie in understanding why the dismissal has happened.

In his study of Chief Executives, Boeker (1992), says that the role of power and influence is key. Dismissals are not only a function of poor performance but are more likely when the Chief Executive does not have much power in the organization. "Power" he argues, comes from the way the organization is structured and the amount of loyalty to the Chief Executive among the other senior managers of the organization. The CEO is less likely to be dismissed by:

- People appointed since the CEO came in (likely to be people with whom the CEO feels comfortable or in his own model).
- When appointees are "insiders" to the organization rather than outsiders.
- When power is spread among a larger rather than smaller number of individuals.
- Where the CEO has some "equity" or ownership of the organization.

If the CEO does have power and is difficult to dismiss even in times of poor performance, than Boeker (1992) argues that sacking one or two managers who report into the CEO may be a credible alternative to getting rid of the CEO. The idea that a CEO needs to be dismissed can amount, he says, to scapegoating.

The phenomenon which Boeker discusses has long been debated in relation to sport. As early as 1964, Gamson and Scotch talked about "scapegoating" in baseball. Craig Brown also found that changing leaders in American Football showed similar characteristics:

> Conventional wisdom holds that changing leaders will improve organizational performance. In contrast, it has either been argued that, because of its disruptiveness, succession will have a negative impact on organizational effectiveness, or that succession has no causal impact and is better viewed as ritual scapegoating. (Brown 1982: 1).

Brown goes on to confirm, that among his sample of coaches who were sacked mid-season in the US American Football leagues from 1970 to 1978:

a ... detailed analysis of within season succession indicates that a dramatic slide in performance leads to one coach's exit, and, under the successor, there is a recovery similar to that in teams that declined steeply but did not dismiss their manager.

In other words, in these sports organizations, the coach is scapegoated but the performance of the team ends up no better or worse than it would have been had the coach stayed. So if there is no impact on performance, why does scapegoating continue to happen?

Bonazzi (1983) reviews the whole issue of scapegoating which is based on work in different areas. From anthropology we learn that:

- the ritual sacrifice of the scapegoat [is] a primary institution of controlling violence symbolically. The group vents its anger symbolically on one of its members.

From sociology, that idea is proposed of:

- a sudden growth of the social need to look for a 'scapegoat on whom one's emotional tension can be relieved. (Moore 1956)

Both of the above are described by Bonazzi as "expressive scapegoats." There is also, however, another type of scapegoat which he describes as the "instrumental" scapegoat. Here, using evidence drawn from Commissions of Enquiry which investigates major disasters comes the idea that the:

laying of blame on an individual level, can be interpreted as a mechanism designed to hide the flaws in the social structure and to distract public opinion. (Bonazzi 1983: 2)

He goes on to suggest that placing the blame on an individual and transforming them into scapegoats "becomes ... an expedient for delaying or avoiding structural changes." (Bonazzi 1983: 2)

There is suggestion that "instrumental scapegoats" might be created within organizational structures precisely so that they can take the rap in the event of something going wrong. Unfortunate though it may be for CEOs, football managers, headmasters and others who seem to be judged on increasingly short timescales, it may well be the case that that, increasingly, they are the fall guys of their respective organizations.

In his 2004 paper, Banning points to the fact that changing CEO often has positive consequences for the financial market, especially when the new incumbent is from the outside of the organization. Changing the leader might well be symbolic scapegoating. And current patterns of changing football manager may well be similar to the scapegoating behavior seen in baseball and American Football.

The impact of turbulence

But what are the effects of repeated changing of leaders? When there is even one change, management theory suggests that there is often little or no benefit for performance. The main reason why theory suggests that changing leader has negative consequences is that it is disruptive. It may create tensions and instabilities among staff who feel that a previous incumbent was harshly treated and who feel that their loyalties are torn. Others argue that leadership has little impact on organizational performance, as the latter is much more influenced by other aspects of the organization (Gamson and Scotch 1964, Lieberson and O'Connor 1972).

The remainder of this chapter examines the case of football, in which management tenure is now less than a year-and-a-half and falling, to see what effect, if any, changes of manager have on performance.

What happens when you change football manager?

In a recent study of managerial changes in the Premier League, Danish journalists at *Tipsbladet* presented data (by Torsten Kjems, 23 February 2009) that describe a "shock effect" of changing manager in the English Premier League. When the average points gained from the last five games before dismissal were compared with those for the five games after dismissal, they argued that there was an uplift or "shock effect" where the average points per game went up from 0.77 points in each game to 1.14 points per match, an increase of 48 percent.

This uplift has varied over time, so for example, in 1992–93, the average points per game for the five games before dismissal was only 0.4 and the average after changing managers was 1.6 points per game, The lowest ever average points before dismissal was in 1995–96 (when managers gained only 0.2 points per game on average before dismissal; the 1998–99 season showed a similarly low performance before managers were dismissed). In some seasons the shock effect has been far less marked than in others.

These data seem, at face value, to suggest that in football, unlike in other sports and other sectors, changing manager might improve performance. The question of whether this is really the case, however, merits further consideration.

Measuring the impact of football manager succession

Popular myth would have it that a football manager is never more than six games away from the sack. Certainly, football managers tend to be dismissed when they have had a poor run of results – although occasionally the trigger may be pulled after a victory or may be prompted by something other than results. In his paper on the timing of dismissal of English Premier League football managers, Chris Hope (2002) talks about this reduction in points and the level at which a manager is dismissed. He argues that there is a bottom level of points (again measured using average points per game), below which a manager will be dismissed. This is the trapdoor.

Similarly, there seems to be a honeymoon period (the same idea as Tipsbladet's shock effect) after a new manager comes into the club. During the honeymoon period the new manager achieves better results than the "steady state" performance achieved by the previous manager. Chris Hope (2002) confirms the existence of a honeymoon period for English football managers. There are many plausible reasons for this honeymoon period. Players may not know whether they are going to figure in the new manager's plans and may be playing to impress. Particularly at the current time, in which the credit crunch has brought a tightening of belts, there is a large market of players without contract who would be keen to step into the shoes of someone who is moved on. Sometimes, the honeymoon may

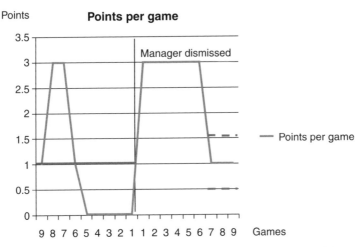

Figure 4.1 Expected pattern of results pre and post sacking of a manager

represent a response from remorseful players who realize that they played a part in the previous manager being sacked. If the player wants to move on, they may be trying to put themselves in the shop window and playing for their own future as well as for the club or manager. If it seems unlikely that players can raise their game so significantly, consider for a moment how many players score on their debut with a new club ...

Using the notion of the "trapdoor" and the "honeymoon period," the run of results before and after a manager is dismissed might be expected to look like an S-curve.

The manager has a decline in performance resulting in dismissal and rises for a time after the new manager is appointed. Before the slump to the trapdoor – and after the honeymoon period – will be some kind of steady state performance.

Hope's model talks about different phases which any football manager's career may go through. These include:

Inspiring   In which the team are inspired by the new appointment and obtain a boost in performance.

Rebuilding   In which performance might drop below normal whilst the manager makes changes and the new team beds in.

Within the normal range of performance Hope (2002) talks about:

Ageing   Where a team may mature within a range of normal performance.

Boosting   Upturns in performance.

Dropping   Downturns in performance.

Decaying   Where a team hits a longer-turn fall towards the trapdoor.

Perhaps not over the total lifespan of every manager, but for a period longer than Tipsbladet's five games before and after dismissal, it is important to look at a football manager's performance over time. If we do not do so, we cannot work out what the steady state performance might look like before and after a change of manager.

For meaningful comparison we might use a standard period of time before and after dismissal. Tipsbladet's five games before and after measurement seems short as the dip down to the trapdoor and the peak gained during the honeymoon are longer than five games. In this case Tipsbladet's "shock effect" is simply a measurement from the bottom of the trough to the tip of the honeymoon upturn, rather than being a real measure of what happens when a football manager is changed.

Variations in performance over time

To demonstrate the way in which we might look at football manager's performance over time, the following section looks at a period of time in Arsenal's football managerial history. Taking Arsenal's data from the beginning of the 1994–95 season, when George Graham was manager through 1995–96 season, when Bruce Rioch was the manager, and spanning 1996–97 when Arsène Wenger was appointed, through to the end of that season, the trend line for results fluctuates as we might expect. Performance is measured in six game blocks using the average points gained in each block. (see Figure 4.2). Hopefully this shows the variation in performance which might naturally happen within a football manager's tenure outside of the trapdoor and honeymoon periods.

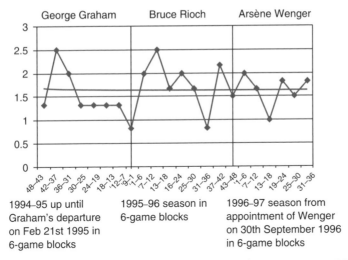

Figure 4.2 Average points per 6-game block from 1994 to 1997

Several important issues are raised by looking at this data.

- Each manager has peaks and troughs in performance over time.
- No average points total for a six-game period ever goes below 0.83 points average or exceeds 2.5 points average. Indeed only two periods ever exceed a points average of 2 per game and two fall below 1 point per game. The majority fall somewhere in a range from 1–2 points per game.
- The average points per game over time across this time period is 1.64 points per game and the trend is fairly stable regardless of the peaks and troughs.
- For this time period, the points averages per manager are:
  - George Graham's average points per game in 1994–95 – 1.5
  - Bruce Rioch's average points per game – 1.79
  - Arsène Wenger's average points per game – 1.64 so, if we judged this too soon we might assume that Arsène Wenger was less successful as a manager than his predecessors, although he was presumably going through a *building* stage as identified by Hope and went on to achieve the highest performance of all.

Table 4.2 The six games before and after the managerial change

Graham to Rioch Block of games	Average points per game
6 – 1	0.83
1 – 6	2.0

Note: Increase in average points per game = 1.17

Rioch to Wenger Block of games	Average points per game
6 – 1	1.5
1 – 6	2.0

Note: Increase in average points per game = 0.5.

If we narrowed down the data range to look at the six games before and after each managerial change we would see the following in Table 4.2.

These increases look like Tipsbladet's 'shock effect' and show a similar increase in performance by changing the manager. In fact, these might well be measurements from the trapdoor to the honeymoon which are shown by the arrows in Figure 4.3 below.

Despite the peaks and troughs within different periods of time, Arsenal's performance did not appear to change dramatically with its changes of managers over this period. There does appear to be a points peak when Bruce Rioch takes charge, and a slightly less dramatic peak when Arsène Wenger takes over.

The trendline (shown in black) suggests, however, that performance is fairly stable over time. If anything, Arsène Wenger's early performance might not appear to have the peaks of the tenure of George Graham and Bruce Rioch. Looking at the points average over the full tenure of George Graham and Arsène Wenger reveals a different picture and shows the dangers of making judgments on a snapshot in time, even one as long as a season.

- George Graham: average points per game – 1.75
- Bruce Rioch: average points per game –1.79
- Arsène Wenger: average points per game – 1.97

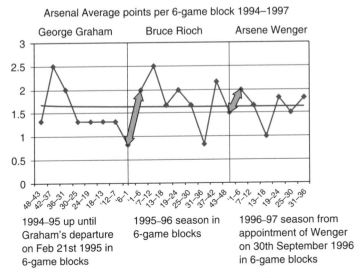

Arsenal Average points per 6-game block 1994–1997

George Graham   Bruce Rioch   Arsene Wenger

1994–95 up until   1995–96 season in   1996–97 season from
Graham's departure   6-game blocks   appointment of Wenger
on Feb 21st 1995 in   on 30th September 1996
6-game blocks   in 6-game blocks

Figure 4.3 Measurement for average points six games before to six games after change of manager

Note: Arrows indicate the increase.

Trapdoors and honeymoon periods

A similar pattern of 'trapdoors' before the departure of a manager and honeymoon period, after the appointment of the next manager, is supported by analysis of the data for other Premier League clubs. So, for example, if we compare the recent management changes at Tottenham Hotspur football club we see the following patterns (Figures 4.4 and 4.5).

Looking at this data we can see that – in general – a manager at Tottenham appears to have had a honeymoon period, shown by a peak of performance after appointment. In some cases – as with the appointment of George Graham, Ossie Ardiles, Gerry Francis, and Harry Redknapp - this has been rapid. In other cases, performance has built to a peak more slowly – as in the case of Martin Jol and Juande Ramos. Sometimes the peak in performance is dramatic and at other times it is less marked. The average pattern for Tottenham before and after a change of manager is shown in Figure 4.6 below.

Interestingly, this suggests that – on average – the honeymoon might not happen until the 7–12-game mark and its effects have

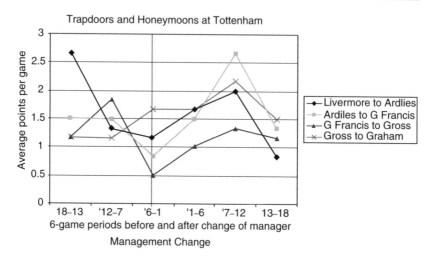

Figure 4.4 The average points performance of Tottenham managers before departure and of new manager after appointment

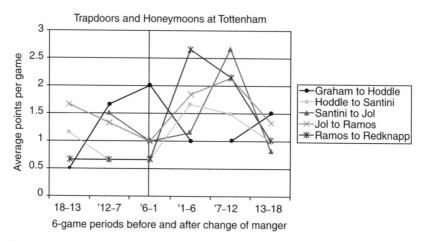

Figure 4.5 The average points performance of Tottenham managers before departure and of new manager after appointment

disappeared by the 18-game mark. In fact, overall, Tottenham's changes of manager leave a slightly lower points average at the 18 games mark (1.16 points per game) than the previous manager was achieving before the decline that resulted in a change of manager. The suggestion that changing manager increases points is not true over the longer-term.

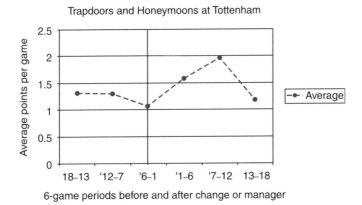

Figure 4.6 Average performance of a Tottenham Hotspur manager before departure and of new manager on appointment

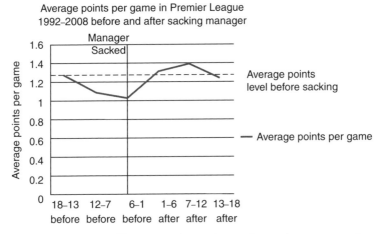

Figure 4.7 What difference does it make when you change manager?

To examine this more fully, this chapter now looks at the data for all management changes within the all Premier League from 1992 to date to see whether this pattern is repeated. To help in understanding the following figures, Appendix 3 shows both the teams who have been in the Premier League from its inception in 1992 and the number of seasons for which their data is included in the total (see Figure 4.7).

So in the Premier League, at least, there is an uplift for a short honeymoon period and then performance dips back to a level slightly below the level where it was before the change of manager. Twelve games after appointment, the points benefit of changing manager has vanished, suggesting that any benefit is very short-lived and the longer-term impact of changing manager is negative.

Looking at the trends over time, it seems both that the peaks and troughs of performance are levelling out – perhaps because other factors such as the quality of players are growing in importance relative to the impact made by any individual manager. Moreover, although the level at which a manager was dismissed seemed little changed between the earlier season and the 2006–07 and 2007–08 seasons, in 2008–09 the trend line is much flatter. It seems that manager performance does not need to decline as much before a football manager in the Premier League is dismissed, as shown in Figure 4.8. The fall back in average points once the honeymoon period is over also seems greater than in earlier seasons. This trend is worth monitoring. If it continues, then the effect of changing manager is not just neutral but has a negative impact on performance except for in the very short-term.

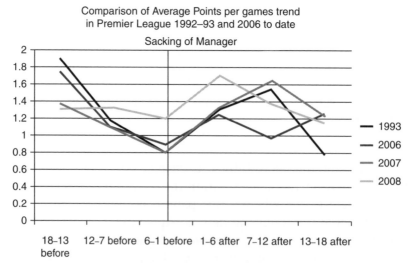

Figure 4.8 Comparison 1992–93 and last three seasons

Conclusion: why changing managers might not work

Overall, changing manager seems to have a negligible effect on how well the club does in the longer-term. Indeed, if we look at the Premier League since 1992, it would appear that – as with other types of organizations – clubs do rather less well once the initial honeymoon period has passed than they did before changing their manager.

If we convert the average points into actual points, a club who dismisses its manager may arrest a decline. Hypothetically if a manager was dismissed 18 games into a season, the club – on average - might gain around 3 points in the 12 game upturn but lose 2 points over the remaining games. A net gain of one point for a considerable outlay and ongoing lower performance. Analysis of club finances – as in Chapter 3 – suggests that spending this money on better players might have a greater effect. In any case, ups and downs of team performance tend to correct themselves over time whether or not a manager is changed. Research from baseball and American Football (Gamson and Scotch 1964, Brown 1982 respectively) suggests that when a coach is not sacked, performance seems to rebound in a pattern similar to that seen in the honeymoon period after a club changes manager. The conclusion seems to be that managerial changes in football do little to improve performance.

Why might this be? Research suggests several possible explanations. The first is that leadership has little impact on organizational performance. Lieberson and O'Connor (1972) suggest organizational performance is more influenced by other aspects of the organizational context such as resources. So perhaps performance might be affected by the quality of players, injuries or just luck rather than anything which the manager does.

The second explanation is that switching to a different leader brings with it disruption which, in itself, can have a negative effect on performance (Grusky 1960, 1963, 1964). Hope (2002) suggests that there are different phases in a football manager's lifespan – in some of which he may have a run of bad luck or a blip and others where performance may take a downturn whilst the manager is rebuilding for the longer term.

This does not mean that a club should never change football manager. As in other organizations, sustained decline in performance is often addressed by changing manager – and this may arrest and turn around performance. The data would suggest, however, that clubs panic and pull the trigger during minor blips in performance rather than following a sustained decline. Moreover, the level at which they do this is getting higher, and the benefits gained from the switch may be less significant than they anticipate.

In any business where there is a high-profile leader figure, it has long been recognized that the "leader" may be scapegoated for poor performance. Leaders are the focus of the uncertainty which affects all organizations. Where the impact of poor performance might place pressure on the Board of the Club, it is perhaps not surprising that there is a temptation to sacrifice the manager. This option is attractive on many levels – the Board can point to its decisive action, the fans have their scapegoat, the new incumbent may be under less pressure to deliver results in the short-term and might thrive as a result. Both the theory and data shown in this chapter suggest, however, that scapegoating of football managers is unlikely to bring an improvement in performance.

CHAPTER 5

Snakes and Ladders

Introduction

This is the way that Lawrie Sanchez described the challenges of building a football management career when speaking at a recent PFA and LMA football manager course. One day you might be riding high, successful and lauded by fans and media, but the next, success can slip away rapidly. A few bad results, eroding confidence, dismissal and then a hard climb back up the ladder. Whilst it may be part and parcel of football management, such ups and downs can be difficult to accept and often difficult to understand. In discussing the ups and downs of Peter Taylor's football management career, the *Observer* ("Football Managers: The Panic Room," *The Observer Sports Monthly*, 6 October 2002) commented how ridiculous decisions to sack a manager can be – Taylor was sacked by Leicester although six months previously when the club were fourth in the league and in the quarter-finals of the FA Cup everyone was saying he was the best manager out and touting him as a potential England manager. Six months later after a run of poor results he was out. In all of his other jobs up until then he had gone as a result of changing circumstances, the ebb and flow of fortunes which is all too common in football.

Given the turbulent nature of football management, such twists and turns (and Peter Taylor's football management career has gone through a few more since then, culminating, most recently, in his parting company with Wycombe Wanderers on 9 October 2009) are an inevitable part of the job.

How then do managers make sense of the rapid and repeated ups and downs of their profession? Whilst press reports often refer to the "football merry-go-round," the opportunity to return to the game they love does not come for all managers. A staggering half of all first-time football managers are never appointed again. The odds get better the more frequently the manager finds another route back into football management. Yet the length of the gaps in between appointments is increasing, more and more out-of-work managers chase every vacancy and dismissals – whether or not they were as a result of anything the manager could control – seem to "count against" managers such that they are re-appointed below the level they had reached before their dismissal. This is not a career for the faint-hearted.

This chapter begins with the challenges of climbing the ladder to a football management career and then considers some of the issues facing managers when they "slide down a snake" through dismissal.

Ladders

The transition from player to manager

You could be a leading figure in football; the captain or leader of the other players, perhaps an acknowledged role model for the younger members of the team, part of the dressing room banter, respected for your "on the pitch" skills and a mover and shaker on the players' social scene. This status only lasts, however, while you are still playing.

Once someone stops playing a number of new challenges arise. What these are depends on the chosen path. Some players move into media, become an agent or retrain for another profession. For some, however, the temptation to remain within the football environment is too great and they begin the transition from player to manager or coach. Sometimes this transition can be sudden and unplanned. Perhaps the manager is sacked and the Chairman offers one of the players the role of caretaker manager. Whilst the player might have thought about making this step at some stage in the future, this might happen much more suddenly than expected – possibly before the player has completed any coaching badges or made any other steps to prepare themselves for the change of role. In other cases, a player might make all the right moves to prepare themselves and not be in the right place at the right time to get an opportunity. The frustration of seeing others who played at the same level getting chances is understandable and it is compounded by the other uncertainties of the transition between playing and coaching. Most football players and other ex-professional sports people feel the loss of status and identity which went with a playing career. This is made worse by the loss of training and matchday routine which may have been part of the footballer's life for twenty years and the lethargy that comes from no longer training.

That this transition is difficult for many football players can be seen in the large number of ex-football players whose marriages break up during the period just after they stop playing, and by a higher than average incidence of drug, alcohol and gambling addictions which fill the void left by playing the game they love. The sports-playing careers of elite athletes inevitably end at a young age and elite sports stars face career transition into either related or unrelated roles. Traditionally football players bought a pub or business and spent the rest of their careers reliving their finest sporting moments. Whether they wish to progress into the coaching and management side of football or else carve out a second career elsewhere, the transition process is increasingly recognized as one which can be traumatic for elite athletes.

Even if the step into coaching and management presents itself quickly, a player may not be prepared for all that comes with stepping across an invisible line into the new role. Will the players be pleased to have 'one of their own' in charge? Sport is essentially competitive and those with a strong competitive spirit are the ones who have thrived. This does not always sit well with watching a fellow player be recognised as a potential leader. The question of "Why him and not me?" might result in tensions and a lack of support among former team mates.

The answer in some cases may be "yes". Friends and colleagues may be supportive and want their mate to succeed. Even so, they will still treat him differently now that he is manager rather than player. The first managerial appointment may happen when a senior player is elevated to coaching or management because of a change in personnel at the club. The manager soon learns that, whilst he got on brilliantly with his team as a player, the rules of engagement are now very different from when he was "one of the lads." Indeed, the manager – player relationship is also different from the relationship he may have had if he had come to management via a coaching role. Whilst it is perfectly acceptable, and probably desirable, for the coach to be close to the players, to put an arm round them or know what is going on in their lives, the manager's relationship needs to be a little more arm's length.

There are a number of reasons why this must be so. First, the manager needs to make decisions on who plays and who should be at the club without being swayed by friendships. He will need to make difficult decisions for the good of the club. It is also hard to get a big picture, strategic overview and to work out how best to achieve success if you are too much in amongst the day-to-day action. It can be difficult to see the "wood from the trees." The manager also needs to gain the respect of his players. Being involved in banter is fine, but what was quite acceptable as a player may not be so for the manager. Being last out of the bar as a player might afford certain kudos, but doesn't look so good in a manager.

Sometimes the players are the first to recognize the new and "invisible" lines which appear once their former colleague has made the step into management. Here are a couple of anecdotes told to me by players who have made this transition:

> The first match after I became caretaker manager, I walked into the dressing room to get changed before the match. I was quite hurt because they all just turned round and looked at me. One of my friends said "you can't get changed in here now. You're the gaffer." They made me go and get changed in the referees' room on my own. I suddenly realized how big a step I'd made and how things would be different from now on.

> I was a bit of a social organizer among the squad. I used to arrange the nights out for the lads. When I was asked to be caretaker manager, I had just arranged for everyone to go out the following week. I wasn't sure whether or not I should still go. Was it acceptable for the manager to go out with the lads? Would I be welcome, or would I now be seen as cramping their

style? In the end, I asked one of the other senior players what he thought I should do. He said I should still come along but I didn't feel very comfortable and don't think they were very relaxed with me there either. I felt like it was the end of an era and it happened overnight.

A number of aspects of "transition" come out of these stories:

- The transition can be unexpected and sudden. The player may have considered being a manager and have done coaching badges, but might not be expecting this to happen yet. They may not have thought through what changes they will need to make or appreciated how differently the players will behave towards them.
- The reality of being a football manager is lonely. There are tough decisions to be made. You are no longer one of a group, but the figure in the spotlight. Depending on how results are going, you can be hero or villain. The plaudits, or fan abuse, will be targeted at the manager much more intensely than at an individual player.
- The manager will inevitably have to build a different relationship with players, even his friends, than he had before. He may even be viewed with suspicion precisely because he *was* one of the group - more so than a manager who comes from outside of the club. The "poacher turned gamekeeper" knows where the players go, if anyone breaks the rules and so on, because he has been there and been part of it.
- Not everyone will find the change in your status easy to deal with. Other senior players may even be jealous – "why pick him not me?" – and perceive the need for distance between you and them more than you do yourself. You have the power to hire and fire and this has changed the relationship between you. One manager was amazed to learn that a player dared not ask "the gaffer" if he could run some coaching sessions. As a young manager not so far from his own playing days, he still felt himself to be approachable and didn't see why the player would hesitate. The player was concerned not to overstep the mark and look pushy to his boss.

Research into second careers among sports stars identifies a number of challenges in the change from playing to coaching or managing:

Planned or unplanned

It is hard to predict and plan for when a playing career might end. Most young people know the end date for the different stages of their education and formulate plans at each stage for what might come next. As with anyone whose career ends suddenly and prematurely – perhaps through redundancy or the company failing – the unexpected nature of the change makes it hard to accept. For sports stars, a career ending injury may mean that the individual has to make this adjustment earlier than planned, might have a sense of being cut off from peers who are still playing or competing in the sport and also can feel a range of emotions such as bitterness or a sense of being cheated out of the career they should have had. Research suggests that the transition process is more difficult for athletes who face "involuntary retirement" than for those who reach the natural end of their sporting career.

Loss of identity

The impact of losing a job which has formed a major part of life is not just financial but also changes "roles, relationships and daily routines" (Stephan and Bilard 2003). Career transition can also bring a psychological impact because of the loss of identity. Adults tend to define themselves and create an identity around their work "I am a lawyer, doctor, businesswoman" and so on. Where this identity is prestigious and attracts the particular admiration of others "I am a football player or Olympic athlete" then coming to terms with the loss of this identity can be problematic. Research by Blinde and Greendorfer (1985) suggests that immersion in sport can be so intense that identity is viewed only in terms of sporting achievement. This can be very positive during a sporting career, but cause difficulty in emotional and social adjustment to the loss of the career and identity once playing days are over. The loss might be compared to a bereavement – with a "hole" being left in the person's life and there is the danger that the loss might be compensated for in unhealthy as well as healthy ways. Kerr and Dachshyn's work in gymnastics (2000) showed that female gymnasts continued to describe themselves in terms of their sport for some time after retirement and found it hard to understand that they were anything other than a gymnast. Warriner and Lavallee (2008) found that gymnasts were distressed by the loss of identity that accompanied the end of their sporting careers.

The work of Martin Roderick (2006), himself an ex-professional football player, reflects both the uncertainty which footballers feel if they are injured and the relationship between "work" and "self". Grint (2005) suggests that work defines how people perceive, define and evaluate themselves. It also plays a big part in self-confidence and self-fulfilment (Bain 2005). Footballers are certainly "special" in the eyes of fans. Roderick (2006) describes this as a an idealization of footballers but goes onto explain that this "specialness" is drummed into players over the years of their careers with a – perhaps unintentional – message that "you are doing something which most people would love to do, you are privileged" and, as a result, you come to believe that you are doing something very much "out of the ordinary." McGillivray *et al.* (2005) describe the sense in which professional footballers are "caught up" in what they do especially as, for many players, "this is the only thing that they have ever done". For many professional footballers, the path towards a playing career may have begun, and shaped their existence from early childhood and have occupied their working lives up until early or mid-30s.

The upside is that this is a fantastic experience while it is happening. The downside is that its loss is then felt more intensely once it has gone. Elite sports people, footballers included, often struggle to adjust to more ordinary occupations in second careers which might not provide the same sense of self-worth or be viewed by others (and themselves) as so prestigious. The feeling of "second best" imbues many comments made by professionals of many sports about their second careers.

Several current football managers have commented that "nothing will ever be quite as good as playing, but managing is the nearest I can get to the feeling." This seems to echo the sense of loss which is found in other sports at the end of a playing career.

Loss of social networks

The idea that employees in particular occupations develop personal contacts and social networks around their employment is not new. As with many other occupations football has a shared workplace culture and ways of interacting with others in the game. McGillivray *et al.* (2005) talk about the way in which the "small world" of football, has its own logic, rules and way of being and behaving. "Is he a football person?" people often ask me. So far as I can tell a "football person" is someone who has gained this status from having played professionally, to a certain standard or maybe this status might be gained from a life long career working in a football club. I have worked in football for close on ten years but sadly seem destined never to achieve this status!

Wacquant (1995) says that the professional footballer is "inhabited by the game he inhabits" (Wacquant 1995: 88). He finds it difficult to see if you take him out of the game and needs football's logic, language and aspirations to shape life.

Making sense of the new role

Although a player might think to themselves that they would like to be a manager, and be pleased when given the opportunity, Gilmore suggests that what they thought it would be like is often very different to expectations. Some of the new managers struggled with the tasks that faced them:

> We led a physical life for as long as I can remember – since 14 years of age. You don't have to use your brain on lots of skilful issues. So when you're suddenly subjected to having to put your mind and body to answering the phone ... to answer letters ... how to handle a secretary ... how much do you want for a player? And those conversations, you haven't got a clue ... there were a multitude of minor things all in that package which you have no idea how to handle, not a clue, not a clue. (Gilmore 2000: 129)

When talking to current managers to understand what skills could be built into coaching and other training courses to help prospective football managers, one manager who got his first job in the early 1990s said:

I got the job and on the first day I showed up and the secretary let me into my office, the manager's office with a phone in and I didn't know where I was supposed to start. I knew about football, I could do the on-the-pitch things, but I had never worked in an office and I just sat there and waited for something to happen but no one came in so after a while I picked the phone and rang my Mum.

What if this does not happen straight away?

There is a fair degree of luck in whether a player will happen to get the opportunity to move straight into coaching or managing. In some cases, despite having done all of the right things, the player will reach the end of their playing time without an immediate opportunity to make the next step.

Other than by appointment as caretaker manager, and in the cases of a lucky few getting appointed at the top end because of their playing name – in itself a mixed blessing given that this might be the one and only chance that they get and it is happening where the scrutiny and pressure is highest – it is not clear how a player will get the opportunity to gain experience as a coach or manager. The old "apprenticeship" model in which a senior player stepped up to help with coaching and became part of the staff is less common than it used to be. As for any young, would-be manager coming through the ranks, jobs are difficult to get without experience – and experience is not always easy to get. An unintended consequence of the churn in football managers is that there is a large pool of available coaches and managers desperate for a route back into the game.

It might almost seem beneficial to create a cadre of "trainee coaches" who might gain experience within football clubs. These posts might become part of the pathway for those players who indicate that they wish to go down this route (perhaps as part of the playing contract). Whilst this is artificial in a way, if every club was encouraged to have a couple of current players – or recently finished players – on the staff, this would help to create a pool of trained and experienced staff coming through the ranks.

Not all players are skilled at signalling their intent to become a manager. It may be that whilst they are playing, they do not wish to contemplate life after playing. It could be that they are not sure in mid career whether this is the career path for them. Players may be reluctant to ask for coaching responsibilities in case it appears that they are trying to "muscle in" on the manager's job. The Board of Directors may not see much of some players and, even if they do, may not perceive them as potential managers:

> The last manager recommended me to be his replacement. I was already working on the coaching staff, but when I went for the interview the CEO said "I never thought of you as a potential manager before, I've only ever seen you on the training pitch wearing a track suit."

Part of the transitional phase, therefore, relates to the training and preparation of prospective football managers.

Training and preparation

Does playing experience help to prepare you as manager?

I think that playing under different managers is very important in your preparation. If you only played for one manager, then what worked for him and that club may not work as your management style, for all manner of reasons. If you played for several, you can compare different managers. What are the common factors about them? What are the differences? What worked and when did you think "I'm never going to do that because I know from the player's side that it just doesn't work." This variety of experience helps you be more discerning about what might work for you before you get into the job. Bear in mind the most powerful lessons you learn are sometimes how NOT to do things rather than, "that worked for him and so I am going to do it."

I think I have taken bits from lots of the managers I have worked with. I might have thought "yes, I really admire that about you" and would aspire to take the calmness under pressure from one, or the passion and enthusiasm from another.

But at the end of the day you can't necessarily be a Wenger or Ferguson, even if they managed you and were great. You might take on parts of how they would handle something, but you need to be your own man rather than try to be someone else.

As suggested in Chapter 3, experience as a player does not necessarily give prospective managers all of the insights and learning that they need to function successfully as a football manager. All the same, there are elements of playing experience that can help. Some players refer to particular lessons they learned as a player and certainly, those players who showed leadership ability and took on roles such as captain, coaching youths, reserves, the strikers and so on, may well have a natural aptitude to lead which would stand them in good stead as a manager. Senior players – leaders on the pitch – will be entrusted with information and instructions for other players and may be used to redress the loss of control which the manager has once the players have stepped over the line onto the pitch. These players would seem to be those most likely to progress on into management, although there are several instances of successful current managers – often those who are more introverted – who did not appear as though they were most likely to follow a path into management.

The player as an apprentice manager model is one which is often referred to by the current generation of successful managers. The idea of being brought in to work alongside the manager is one which works well from both sides. The manager gains players with a real insight into his challenges who might well be able to communicate these to other players and reinforce messages, as well as carrying out is wishes on the pitch. The player gets a sense of what it is really like to be a football manager and might work out whether it would be right for him. Of course, this relationship takes trust on both sides so may only work in certain situations.

Pathways to management

In contrast to the "shock," which faces managers who were catapulted suddenly into the role, the end of an athletic career might well be anticipated and be something for which the athlete plans. Perhaps there is a recurrent injury, which it seems might bring about the end of a playing career, perhaps a lack of first team opportunities, or a steadily downward trend in the clubs on offer.

In this kind of situation, an elite sports player might begin to make preparations for what comes next. This kind of preparation may begin early. A number of the currently successful managers did their coaching badges at a relatively young age. Tony Pulis did his his UEFA Full Badge, then the highest coaching qualification, at age 21. Aidy Boothroyd had his coaching badges up to level A and coaching qualifications by his mid 20s. On his appointment at Watford at the age of 34 in 2005, he said that he had been working towards this moment for a long time.

As the route into football management professionalizes, with the considerable efforts of the PFA, FA and LMA, there are a clear set of coaching badges, courses and stages which players need (or are advised) to complete in order to prepare themselves to make the transition. As John Barnwell, Chief Executive of the League Managers Association, explained in 2005:

> Stability is invariably the key to success in any industry and football is no different. The LMA believes it is crucial that our members are given every possible opportunity to succeed at their clubs. We also feel it is vitally important that our members are prepared as best as they possibly can be when they take up managerial appointments. Our association has introduced a package of benefits and qualifications, which we believe helps managers to cope with the diverse challenges they face as managers. (http://www2.warwick.ac.uk/newsandevents/pressreleases/footballmanagers100106)

When announcing the launch of a football management course to sit alongside the UEFA coaching badges offered by the Football Association, PFA Chief executive Gordon Taylor said "The role of the modern football club manager has changed considerably ... the high profile nature of the industry now requires that players considering a career in football management will need high quality management training."

Then Football Association Technical Director (now Chairman of the League Managers Association) Howard Wilkinson said:

> Football is investing heavily in coaching and playing skills so that we can match the rest of the world. We are looking to take management skills into the boardroom and bootroom to create a similar revolution. (http://www.wbs.ac.uk/news/releases/2002/05/17/Warwick/Business/School)

Whilst it is impossible to recreate the value of experience – which is known to add to the likelihood of football manager success particularly in higher leagues, preparation to support the transition from football playing to football coaching or management – for those who choose to follow this route for a second career. This helps players to identify whether they are well suited to the career and to prepare in advance for the challenges of the role.

Progression

The option of starting at the bottom of the leagues and working up may be less common than it used to be, but there are still several instances of managers who have done well in lower leagues and progressed upwards. Please note that a move is counted as a progression if the manager resigned, or did not renew his contract, in favor of another club and does not necessarily imply that the club to which the manager moves is higher placed or a "step up." Sometimes managers might move to manage their boyhood club or for other reasons rather than to move up the leagues. Table 5.1 shows management progressions since 1992.

Whilst progressions up the leagues remained low throughout the 1990s and the early 2000s, the rate appears to be on the increase once more – with seven in 2006, seven in 2007 and four so far in 2009–10. These are almost all between the Football Leagues, although a few – such as Paul Ince to Blackburn and Roberto Martinez to Wigan – involve progression into the Premier League. It is hoped that the upturn in progressions may help managers to see routes whereby they can gain experience

Table 5.1 Managers progressing since 1992

Year	Progressions
1993	2
1994	4
1995	4
1996	0
1997	4
1998	4
1999	2
2000	3
2001	3
2002	4
2003	3
2004	5
2005	2
2006	7
2007	7
2008	4
2009	4

and then be rewarded by getting higher league jobs. Whether this results in longer average tenure of managers is not yet clear, and certainly the short time given to Paul Ince at the higher level might seem to cast doubt on this.

Snakes

Resignation and enforced absence through illness

In October 2001, the health implications of pressurized management rules were brought sharply into focus with the shocking heart problems suffered by the Liverpool manager, Gerard Houllier, during a match with Leeds United. Houllier later admitted he had been worried about his health for some time but had not wished to show there was anything wrong. He is a self-confessed workaholic (Sunday, 6 October 2002, *Observer Sport Monthly*). Despite these problems, Houllier returned to work as soon as he felt able.

In recent years, there have unsuprisingly been a number of resignations which are not linked to progression, or else to disagreement with a club, but are prompted by personal or health reasons (see Table 5.2).

Table 5.2 Manager dismissals and resignations, 1992–93 to date

Season[1]	Manager dismissals	Manager total resignations	Progressions	Other resignations	Average tenure dismissed managers (years)
1992–1993	29[2]	2	2	0	3.12
1993–1994	38	4	4	0	2.30
1994–1995	44	7	4	3	2.55
1995–1996	35	8	0	8	2.33
1996–1997	38[3]	4	4	0	2.42
1997–1998	33	7	4	3	1.81
1998–1999	38	5	2	3	1.68
1999–2000	37	3	3	0	2.04
2000–2001	41	5	3	2	2.13
2001–2002	53	10	4	6	2.04
2002–2003	31	4	3	1	2.02
2003–2004	38	8	5	3	2.08
2004–2005	34	5	2	3	2.23
2005–2006	40	7	7	0	1.84
2006–2007	46	11	7	4	2.04
2007–2008	31	10	4	6	1.53
2008–2009	33	12	4	8	1.47

The last couple of seasons have witnessed a marked rise in the number of resignations compared to the earlier seasons. Whilst these include progressions, a number are either for personal reasons and ill health or else appear to take the form of a break or "sabbatical" from football management.

The concept of a sabbatical (from Latin *sabbaticus*, from Greek *sabbatikos*, from Hebrew *shabbat* – that is, Sabbath means a "ceasing") is a rest from work, or a temporary break which may last from two months to a year. This has biblical roots, for example in Leviticus 25, which presents a commandment to stop working in the fields for the seventh year. This idea is still used in the academic field, where academics may have short-term release from teaching, administrative and pastoral duties so that they can focus on larger-scale research projects or broaden their experience by working in other countries and developing communities of scholars. As an idea, the break from routine duties or a step back in the form of a career break is gaining in popularity in other fields.

A rising number of football managers take a short break from the intensity of football management – such as Gordon Strachan from Southampton or Alan Curbishley from Charlton – perhaps because of the pressures of the permanent media spotlight, or higher levels of financial security which make this possible. That this is a feature more at the higher level may reflect the confidence of those who have succeeded at the highest level for an extended period to step away. In the dog-eat-dog world of the Football League, the wish to step back might be inhibited by worries of disappearing for too long and maybe not getting another chance.

Dismissals

The rate at which football managers are dismissed is without parallel in other sectors. Almost half of all managers change jobs every season. Tenure is also declining – it now stands at less than a year-and-a-half on average, as shown in Figure 5.1. The extreme attrition rate of football managers is almost now accepted as being "the nature of the business." Indeed for those

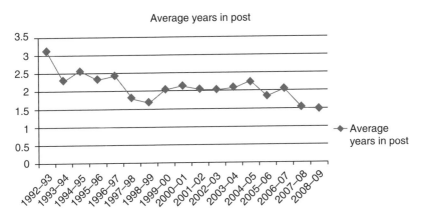

Figure 5.1 Average football manager tenure

whose livelihoods and loved ones are not jeopardized by being directly involved, the sacking of football managers has become almost a sideshow in its own right.

Closer examination of football manager statistics shows some scary trends. As discussed in the introduction to this book, there have been 872 football managers since 1992. Whilst some clubs have been stable – Manchester United have had just one manager, Arsenal three, and Middlesbrough, Liverpool and Crewe have had only four – in the same time period, some clubs have had 14 or 15 managers.

This section explores in greater detail the trends in football manager dismissals and reappointments, as well as discussing the impact of dismissals on managers. For the purposes of this analysis, departures are split between manager dismissals and resignations. Resignation is used to describe situations where managers moved on to another post, have left for personal reasons or on grounds of ill health or retire or step back temporarily from the post. Mutual consent is counted here as a contractual term but still dismissal unless it is clear that the manager wished to leave.

The data show an upward trend in manager dismissals between 1992–93 to date (see Table 5.2 and Figure 5.2). The upward trend is marked between 1992 and 2001–02 with peaks in 1993–95 and again in 2001–02. After the peak in 2001–02, which coincided with the collapse of ITV Digital and the fall out for clubs

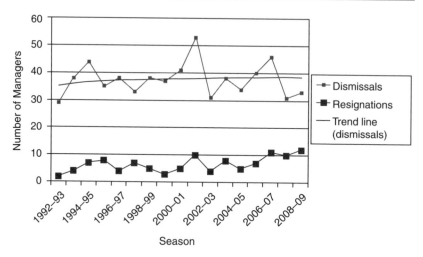

Figure 5.2 Football manager dismissals and resignations, 1992 to date

in the Football League, the rate of dismissals fell back – perhaps as clubs tried to regain some stability.

The 40 dismissals in 2005–06 and 46 in 2006–07 were a return to these high levels of dismissals – the number of dismissals in 2006–07 being the second highest since 1992 – although this fell back to 31 in 2007–08 and 33 in 2008–09. Alongside the number of dismissals is an increase in the number of resignations, some for positive reasons – as managers progress up the league structure – but others as managers take a temporary break from the pressures of management or resigned for personal or ill health reasons. Overall, the picture is one of extreme levels of turbulence and shortening football manager tenure.

Dismissals by league

When dismissals and resignations are split by league, major variations can be seen over time and between leagues. Table 5.3 compares data from 1992–93 with those from 2000–01 to date to find out if these are split equally across leagues, or affect some leagues more than others.

Table 5.3 Number of football management dismissals by league 1992–93 compared with 2000–01 to date

League	1992–1993	2000–2001	2001–2002	2002–2003	2003–2004	2004–2005	2005–2006	2006–2007	2007–2008	2008–2009
Prem	5	7	10	5	4	5	3	8	7	4
CC	9	15	11	7	6	12	11	14	9	8
1	8	16	11	8	10	7	13	14	6	14
2	11	13	23	12	18	10	13	11	9	7

2000–01 and 2001–02 show a sharp rise in dismissals out-side of the Premiership. 2000–01 shows a much larger rise in the rate of dismissals of managers in the middle two divisions and a lower proportional increase in the Premiership and lowest divi-sion. During the 2001–02 season, the deepening financial crisis in football placed particular pressure on the 72 clubs below the Premiership and culminated, in March 2002, in the collapse of ITV digital. The resultant spate of clubs going into administration may explain the increase in dismissals outside the Premiership. The number of dismissals dips as the crisis settled but remains higher for the three lower leagues than for the Premiership.

The 2004–05 seasonsaw a particular increase in dismissals in the Championship which has continued until 2007 although it has fallen back somewhat in recent seasons. The relatively high dismissals in this league may come from pressure on managers to reach the golden prize of promotion to the Premiership.

Management merry-go-round?

It is popularly supposed that managers continue to recycle into further football manager jobs even when they are dismissed or resign. In fact there is a significant rate of attrition with many first-time managers not being appointed to a second football manager job. Almost half of all first-time managers are never reappointed to a manager's job. This high fall out continues with over a quarter of those who get a second job then going out of management and a further 37 percent of third-time managers not being reappointed (as shown in Table 5.4).

This is not the picture of the "merry-go-round" which sounds like a benign shift around of roles between an established pool of football managers. Perhaps it is more akin to an aggressive form of musical chairs with chairs being snatched out from underneath managers who have barely had a chance to sit down. The reality is one of very high levels of "churn" with an ever new supply of young and inexperienced managers coming in at the bottom end and few surviving to learn from their experiences to become bet-ter managers. If this "churn" were experienced in other sectors, serious concern would be raised either at the calibre of the talent pool or at the recruitment and assessment process.

Table 5.4 Manager exits

Times managed	Percentage exits to appointees
One	49.07
Two	28.47
Three	37.36
Four	34.43
Five	32.5
Six	48.15
Seven	50.0
Eight	85.71
Nine	
Ten	

The average length of time which it takes a dismissed football manager to get another football managers job is around one and a half years. Sometimes a manager may actively choose not to look for another football manager's job – choosing instead to work in an Academy, as an assistant manager or in a role outside of football. Typically, however, this period elapses while a manager seeks another position, given that each job attracts a large number of qualified and experienced applicants. At any point in time, a number of high-profile managers are out of employment. At the current time (January 2010), Lawrie Sanchez, Steve Coppell, Iain Dowie and Alan Curbishley, all of whom have recent Premier League experience, are not working.

Implications of the sack race

In talking about dismissal, football managers often speak of different phases which they go through in coming to terms with being sacked. Sometimes, when the hectic schedule of the manager is suddenly ended, the feeling may be of disorientation – what do I do now? Many of the manager's activities, networks of contact and status are tied up in the role which is suddenly – and often unexpectedly – taken away. "For the first week, my phone was red hot. People kept ringing me to say they were sorry to hear the news. Then after a couple of weeks it went quiet."

> I can speak from experience in saying that being sacked was a crushing blow. If kept in perspective though, it can be a massive learning curve. All the elements that go into being successful were in place and – especially if it was your first job, you can learn and grow from it. I certainly think it helped when I managed again.

For any manager who leaves a job involuntarily, the adjustment period is very stressful and managers run a whole gamut of emotions. If this was unexpected, there may be shock. If it feels undeserved, anger. If it has been very pressurized then possibly, relief. As one manager explained:

> For the first couple of weeks I just felt relieved. I was glad to be away from the pressure. I didn't miss it, I was just glad to be away from the situation, to stop hitting my head against a wall. I spent time with my family, time which I hadn't had, caught up on things I should have done and wanted to do. But after a while I didn't know what to do with myself. I am used to being involved in something physical. I needed to get out and put my football boots on, get back to the training ground environment. After all I have spent most of my life in that world.

The feeling that there are other things that the manager has not been able to do is not uncommon. Even going on holiday with the family is something which the manager might not have had time for. School holidays clash with pre-season and the beginning of the football season. Taking the opportunity to get away also takes the manager from the media attention to their dismissal for a while. In any sector where the manager has had a 24/7 role, the chance to catch up with family and friends, to engage in hobbies and pastimes, to learn new skills and do things which are developmental might provide a useful relief.

I must have the tidiest garage in the whole area! For a while it was great to have time to get turned around, but then after a while what do you do?

The sense of loss can, however, be profound. Depending on the circumstances, leaving a job involuntarily might stop the manager from enjoying this unexpected break. Maybe the dismissal felt unfair, or else perhaps the process of reaching an agreement on compensation is protracted or difficult. In more than one case, the news that the manager had been sacked was released into the media before the manager himself had been told. Sometimes when the manager was told by press that he was supposed to have been sacked and had rung the Chairman for confirmation, this was even denied, although it later turned out to be true. When going to meet the Chairman, one manager even saw his replacement – someone he knew – waiting in his car in the car park ready to take over. In some cases, the replacements had moved into the managers office before the previous incumbent even knew they were going or had removed their personal belongings.

Bitterness is not uncommon among sacked football managers:

We knew that the finances were tight and the Chairman had said that he would accept that our league position might suffer in the transition, provided we didn't go below a certain point in the league. So we did that and were getting everything sorted out and we weren't below that league position but I was sacked anyway. That didn't feel fair.

Sometimes there is almost a mourning for the football world, which the manager might feel he has "lost":

It is strange. I am entirely surrounded by women. My wife, daughters. There are only me and the dog who are male. I'm just used to working in a man's world and being surrounded by men. It just feels very strange.

The period between jobs may increasingly be extended and, as there are now often upwards of 50 qualified applicants per vacancy, stands to get longer.

No matter how difficult it is to accept – and anyone who has been made redundant will know that anger, grief and even depression may be stages on the route towards acceptance that life has to move on – this is sadly a process which the football manager is likely to face several times in a career, regardless of how successful they are. This may even be a profession where a "Plan B" – what will I do if I don't get back in, or in those periods between posts – becomes part of the preparations which a football manager must make.

Conclusions

Football management is an exceptionally turbulent profession. Popular opinion sees this as a "merry-go-round" in which a pool of the same faces cycle between jobs. The reality, however, is very different. Attrition rates are high, few managers survive long enough to learn from experience and progress through the career and managers may need alternative career options to cover periods when they go out of management, particularly as such a high proportion go out of the game altogether. For those who do make it, the current turbulence poses challenges in finding and keeping jobs, and in finding opportunities to progress. This may be an extreme case, more snakes and ladders than a merry-go-round, but it highlights a number of features which may also be challenges for many managers in recessionary times and as young potential managers continue to come in at the bottom end of professions.

CHAPTER 6

Final Thoughts on Football Management

As a metaphor for management in general, football management highlights some of the issues facing managers under the spotlight. This final section reviews each of the themes which are covered in the book in turn and then discusses how these might relate to management more broadly.

Football manager as leader

Leadership theory is divided between those who believe that the characteristics and behavior of the individual "visionary" leader are vital to the success of the organization and those who believe that the organizational context determines the success of the organization to a greater extent than the individual. Among those who argue for the role of the individual, there are different views as to whether it is individual characteristics, behavior or visionary abilities which best determine who will be the most successful leaders. Among context factors, organisational structure, finances and the availability of resources play a large role in creating a climate for success.

The specific situation of the football manager is that he must manage in situations which are pressurized, results-driven and where timescales are getting shorter. Football managers are not always judged on actual success but on a perception of how successful they have been that is gained from the media, fans and other commentators on the game. Worryingly, good and bad press may even color the impressions of potential employers whose impressions might also be gained second hand.

The importance of context factors has also emerged for other types of leaders. Whilst individual abilities are clearly important in success, context views suggest that resource availability – both financial and in terms of skilled personnel – play an important role in today's organizations. Football managers' ability to manage talented individuals, as well their drive, passion and resilience, appear as important attributes for leaders in sectors outside of as well as within football.

It is essential that football managers are comfortable in dealing with media and fans. To survive they need to develop the ability to handle relationships with a broad set of stakeholders, managing upwards to the Board of Directors being among the most critical of these. The emotional intelligence which this requires is also emphasized by management theory as key to success for leaders in all types of organizations. It is not only what you do but how you do it which will contribute to success. You cannot be a leader unless others are prepared to follow you.

It seems also that different clubs at different stages of development may require different abilities such as building, revitalizing, turning around organizations or taking over a successful organization and enhancing it without making unnecessary changes. Not all managers may be suited to all of these roles, although it would appear that the attributes of football managers – competitive spirit, passion for the job, resilience and a willingness to work hard – were helpful in all stages of football club lifecycle. Other attributes, such as the ability to build a team anew on a limited budget, or a more generalist compared with a more specialist role might be better suited to some individuals than to others. A common debate in management theory is that of whether certain types of specialists are less likely to succeed as general manager or CEO but might be better suited to becoming head of a particular function (such as information systems or finance). All of the evidence from football management suggests that there is no truth in the belief that a certain specialism – striker rather than defender – determines who would succeed. The potential to become a good leader exists in all functional areas and appears to relate more to individual and personality characteristics and preferences rather than to the nature of functional expertise.

Success and the football manager

Whilst there is no doubting the importance of the charismatic leader figure, context also appears to play an important role in determining the success of the football manager. Success might appear to be simple to judge in a "results-based" business and football managers freely admit that they should be "judged on results." It is possibly too simple for football managers to believe this mantra without fully recognising how great a relationship there is, for example, between the finances of a club and the level at which they might reasonably be expected to achieve. A football manager might over-achieve for a period of time – and indeed some of those discussed in Chapter 3 have done so for extended periods of time – regardless of the players at his disposal. We should, however, recognise the magnitude of these over-achievements rather than raising the bar and sacking the manager if he is not able to repeat this performance continuously. Success in football management can be dangerous and might lead to unrealistic and ultimately impossible demands on the manager.

It becomes apparent that success, even in football, is complex. Much of success is determined by the context. Success may not be judged on actual results but on perceived success. Moreover, the style in which victories are gained can be criticised by fans and boards, even if to play open and attractive football against teams with better players might result in spectacularly entertaining defeats. What to do for the best? This is perhaps not, after all, simply a results business!

Football Managers with certain levels of experience or types of playing reputations and skills seem more or less able to manage at different levels. The data in this book suggest that someone who has experience will be better able to manage at the top level – perhaps because they are better able to handle the egos of top players or because they are better able to handle the pressures, having dealt with these over a period of years. This should not be a surprise to us. Who would expect an inexperienced candidate to be able to step into the Chief Executive's role without learning – and making mistakes – along the way? The difficulties of gaining opportunities and experience in football management sharpen our focus on the best method of qualifying and preparing prospective managers. How to identify high profile candidates and to develop their abilities are challenges which have taxed and continue to tax generations of human resource departments. In the talent economy, these challenges become ever more important, as do the issues of when to retain and when to let go key personnel.

Football manager as talent manager

Among the key challenges for the football manager is that of identifying good players – often gems who have been missed by competitors. Depending on the level at which the football manager operates, this may mean long hours spent travelling the length of the country to attend reserve and youth team matches as well as having "an eye" for something in a player which others may have missed.

The ability to develop a raw talent – and to bring the best out of talented individuals who might not always be the easiest to manage – is also a key attribute of a football manager. The decision to bring in talent which needs to be developed – presumably for a cheaper initial outlay – compared with a player who has already developed their skills – for a higher price – is not always easy. Moreover, a potentially talented player may not always realize their potential, particularly given the rate of attrition among football managers. It may well be that the manager who spotted, and was in the process of building rapport and developing, the player, is no longer in post when the player matures. This may mean either that the next incumbent does not recognize, or perhaps succeed in nurturing, the talent and the value of the investment is lost as the player moves on to another club where he feels more valued.

Making decisions to let go of players who are still at the top is a key facet of successful talent managers. Although these are brave decisions and – if the manager is not secure in his role – may be subject to criticism by others, this is both a means of realizing value from mature talent which can be reinvested in future talent and may keep the team constantly fresh.

These attributes are often referred to among the deciding factors in what makes managers such as Sir Alex Ferguson and Arsène Wenger great.

The challenge of getting the best out of players where there is a large pool of available talent within a club is also under-estimated. It is easy to assume that it is easier for managers in this situation, compared with those who do not have the resources to attract enough talent, but the football manager in this situation will need to address issues such as:

- *Deciding on the best line-up.* The true ability of a player to deliver under the pressure of match day might only be seen by providing playing opportunities. The top player might perform best on a big stage and ability might be hard to judge in a reserve match. The football manager might find it difficult to test out all permutations of players over a sufficient number of matches to be clear on the best combination of talent. Fans and media will presumably also have opinions and may exert pressure on the manager for being unable to decide (implicit in the name Tinkerman for Claudio Ranieri), or for diverging from their preferred players.
- *Whether, how frequently and in what numbers he should rotate talent.* Where the new line-up does well, for example, with Arsenal's youthful cup team last season, then this might be hailed as a good approach, but when changes result in a poorer than usual performance, it can lead to criticism of the manager.
- *How to keep happy the players who are not currently in the first team.* Any club needs sufficient talented players that they can cover for injuries, suspensions and other eventualities. Yet talented players like to be in the spotlight and may have big egos which do not respond well to feeling undervalued. It may be difficult to motivate players who are the second choice for a position and the manager will need to work out how best to make these players feel motivated and appreciated.

All of these challenges also appear in other knowledge-based organizations. The analogy of tinkering with a formation, having a disgruntled reserve team or where cover is needed, enhance our clarity on the types of challenges facing most organizations of this type. Indeed "the leader as a talent manager" is an area in which the metaphor of the football manager works particularly well in helping us to understand the issues.

Football manager succession

Changing football manager – and probably by inference changing manager in any sector – might be seen as a way of improving performance. Certainly, if for whatever reason the organization has the wrong person in charge, then steps may need to be made to address this. Given the frequency with which this happens in football – and given that the manager is most often dismissed after only a short time by the same people who made the appointment – it would appear either that the football manager was the right appointment (but is being held wrongly accountable for performance which anyone would struggle to deliver) or that the process of appointment is flawed in some way that allows repeated appointment of individuals who cannot deliver to the expected level.

Whichever is the case, changing football manager would only appear to improve performance in the short-term and appears even to worsen performance over the longer term. Clubs with greater stability do better than those who chop and change their managers repeatedly. This reinforces the importance of appointing the right individuals with appropriate abilities. These appointments then need time in which to reach steady state and it is unhelpful not just to the manager, but to the future performance of the organization to panic and pull the trigger during a blip in performance. Such downturns most often rectify themselves under the current manager.

Shared goals and realistic evaluation of whether these are being achieved is helpful to all businesses but it is understandably hard to keep confidence in a manager in the face of doubting fans and media speculation. In this area it would appear that football has more to learn from business, than football from business. Proper preparation, transparent recruitment, and performance reviews within the organization rather than in media and elsewhere in the public domain would be more likely to yield the desired results.

Managing in a turbulent market

In summary, the world of the football manager is uniquely pressurized and is characterized by high levels of turbulence. Whilst the extreme highs and lows, the rapid rises and equally rapid falls from grace may be greater than those seen in other sectors, these raise two important issues.

The first issue is for football itself. How can steps be made to slow down the rates of attrition in football management either by better preparation and selection of prospective managers or by better selection and support from the clubs that employ them? It is clear that the current rapid succession of managers is not beneficial to clubs in the long-term and it has implications for building successful teams and culture within the club as well as having financial implications taking money out of the game.

The second is for business managers who identify in football managers some aspect of their own careers and issues. What can we learn from the football metaphor about successful talent management, coping under pressure, dealing with the spotlight, the importance of managing relationships with all of the key stakeholders in our particular world? It would seem that a number of parallels exist between football management and leaders in many of today's organizations:

- Decisions on developing or buying talent. The costs and benefits of taking risks on future potential rather than buying already developed talent.
- The need for systems for early identification of talent. In competitive markets, successful talent managers may be those who identify excellent players that larger rivals have not even heard of.
- Training and development of talent – at all levels of seniority. Talent managers do not only need to develop excellent "players" but also excellent "backroom" staff who work with the leader.
- How to get talented individuals to perform as a team when these individuals – almost by definition – might not be team players.
- How best to use resources flexibly – the need to have some "utility players" alongside excellent specialists.

- The importance of the visionary leader in this process as well as recognition that success may be favored or constrained by availability of resources and other attributes of the organizational context.
- The need for sufficiently long timescales that "steady state" performance can be judged rather than short-term "shock effects" or blips.
- Recognition that "snakes" are increasingly to be found in many sectors and that the ability to work towards and locate the next ladder are essential for potential leaders.

As concluded by both successful football and business managers at the LMA's inaugural management conference in late 2009, both football and management have things to learn from each other. The football analogy gives business useful metaphors to talk about talent management, team building, leadership and even issues such as sacking and second careers. Spare a thought, though, for those who inhabit the world of football management and for whom this is not a mere game and diversion, but their livelihood. In the words of one football manager after his harsh dismissal earlier this season:

> For the first week, my phone was red hot. People kept ringing me to say they were sorry to hear the news. Then after a couple of weeks it went quiet.

This is a book for managers about football, but it is also a book for football about what they could learn from broader management. No sector could survive without damage the level of turbulence in football management and all the evidence from management theory and best practise indicate that it also has a negative impact on the performance of organizations.

Notes

Introduction   The Football Management Context

1. **Premier League:** 11 departures of which 7 (Keane, Curbishley, Keegan, Redknapp, Sbragia 1, Hiddinck 2, Kinnear 3) resigned. 4 managers – Ramos (Tottenham), Ince (Blackburn), Scolari (Chelsea), Adams (Portsmouth) were dismissed.
   Championship: 10 departures of which 2 (Simon Grayson, Blackpool and Steve Coppell, Reading) resigned. 8 managers – Dowie (QPR), Boothroyd (Watford), Pardew (Charlton) Calderwood (Nottingham Forest), Jewell (Derby), Roeder (Norwich), Poortvliet (Southampton), Sousa (QPR) were dismissed.
   League 1: 15 departures of which 1 (Turner, Hereford) resigned. Ternent (Huddersfield) Wilson (Hartlepool), McAllister (Leeds), Holland (Crewe), Williams (Colchester), Downing (Cheltenham), Ward (Carlisle), Malpass (Swindon), Mullen (Walsall), Adams (Brighton), Ling (Leyton Orient), Sheridan (Oldham), Slade (Yeovil) all dismissed. Gannon made redundant, which is counted here as dismissal rather than resignation.
   League 2: 9 departures of which 2 (Paul Fairclough, Barnet and Penney, Darlington) resigned. Buckley (Grimsby), Davies (Chester), Bond (Bournemouth), Sinnott (Port Vale), Quinn (Bournemouth), Glover (Port Vale), Richardson (Chesterfield) dismissed.
2. Sbragia appointed on 18-month contract but resigned at end of season.
3. Kinnear counted as resignation on the grounds of ill health.
4. Hiddinck appointed until end of season. Contract expired. Counted as resignation rather than dismissal.
5. Royle was contracted to the end of the season so is neither a dismissal nor resignation.

Chapter 3   The Golden Boys

1. Crystal Palace, Colchester United, Luton Town do not report their wage data separately. Middlesbrough data are missing for the 2004–05 season. Where managers have managed in lower leagues

(e.g. Brian Laws at Scunthorpe in League 2 and League 1), data are not available for these seasons.

2. Averaged between two clubs managed in this year.

3. Wigan had a caretaker manager when this was written and, for the purposes of Table 3.8, is not included in manager list or percentages.

4. There were 22 teams in the Premier League in the 2002–03 season

5. Where a manager managed in more than one division, the division in which the manager was appointed is used here.

6. John Barnes managed in Scotland and the Jamaican national team, but is counted here as a first-time manager in England. If this were total managerial experience, he would count as a third-time manager.

7. Gullit managed first as player manager at Chelsea and then at Newcastle and went on to manage Feyenoord 2004–05. His third management appointment is not included in these figures.

Chapter 5   Snakes and Ladders

1. Season taken from 1 June to following 31 May in line with LMA convention.

2. One manager changed from dismissal to resignation compared with earlier versions of statistics based on new information.

3. Amendment of dismissals and resignations split based on new information.

Glossary of Football Terms

Football   This is used to describe the game of football played in Europe, Latin America and Asia, rather than American Football. The US would refer to this as "soccer."

League Structure   English football is divided into four leagues, or competitive groups of clubs, who play matches against each other.

The Leagues are:

Premier League   The highest level of English football, the top league. There are 20 teams – although in its first two years of formations (1992–93 and 1993–94) the league contained 22 teams – and each team plays the others twice, home and away during a season to make up 38 matches.

Championship   The second level or league in English football, the Coca Cola sponsored Championship comprises 24 teams, so has 46 matches.

League 1   The third level of English football. Again this has 24 teams so 46 matches per season.

League 2   The fourth level of English football. As with League 1, there are 24 teams and 46 matches per season.

Season   Matches are played over a period from early August of one year through to the following May. The football season is just over 8 months long.

Promotion   The leagues are not closed. At the end of the season, in all leagues below the Premier League the top two teams and one other who wins an end-of-season competition (the play offs) for the remaining place, go up to the level above for the following season. Every season two teams (the Champions and play-off winner) will also enter the leagues from the fifth level known as the Conference Premier League).

Relegation   Conversely, the bottom three teams in the league (four from League 1 and two from League 2, the fourth level) will be relegated, or go down, to the level below for the following season.

Competitive balance   Economists use the term competitive balance to describe the ability of any team within a league to stand an equal chance of beating any other team within that league.

Parachute payment   When teams are relegated from the highest league (the Premier League) the Premier League makes a payment for the first two seasons to help the team to adjust its player wage bills down to the lower levels needed to survive in the Championship.

Appendices

Appendix 1 Club wage ranking compared with manager finishing position

2007/08 Championship	Manager	Difference
Sheff Utd	Bryan Robson	−15
Sheff Utd	Kevin Blackwell	−8
Charlton	Alan Pardew	−9
West Bromwich Albion	Tony Mowbray	2
Watford	Aidy Boothroyd	−2
Southampton	George Burley/ Nigel Pearson	−13
Southampton	Nigel Pearson	−15
Leicester	Martin Allen	−3
Leicester	Ian Hollway	−6
Leicester	Gary Megson	−16
Hull	Phil Brown	4
Wolves	Mick McCarthy	1
Norwich	Glenn Roeder	−8
Cardiff	Dave Jones	−2
Ipswich	Jim Magilton	3
Stoke	Tony Pulis	10
Crystal Palace	Neil Warnock	8
Coventry	Iain Dowie	−7
Coventry	Chris Coleman	−15

(Continued)

2007/08 Championship	Manager	Difference
QPR	John Gregory	−4
QPR	Luigi De Canio	1
Burnley	Steve Cotterill	3
Burnley	Owen Coyle	3
Preston North End	Alan Irvine	2
Bristol City	Gary Johnson	14
Sheff Wed	Brian Laws	3
Plymouth	Ian Holloway	13
Plymouth	Paul Sturrock	10
Blackpool	Simon Grayson	2
Scunthorpe	Nigel Adkins	−1

2007/08 Premier League	Manager	Difference
Chelsea	José Mourinho	−1
Chelsea	Avram Grant	−1
Manchester United	Alex Ferguson	1
Arsenal	Arsène Wenger	0
Liverpool	Rafael Benitez	0
Newcastle	Sam Allardyce	−12
Newcastle	Kevin Keegan	−13
Portsmouth	Harry Redknapp	−2
Manchester City	Sven Goran Eriksson	−2
Tottenham Hotspur	Martin Jol	−10

(*Continued*)

2007/08 Premier League	Manager	Difference
Tottenham Hotspur	Juande Ramos	−3
Aston Villa	Martin O'Neill	3
Everton	David Moyes	5
Blackburn	Mark Hughes	4
Fulham	Lawrie Sanchez	−4
Fulham	Roy Hodgson	−5
Bolton	Sammy Lee	−2
Bolton	Gary Megson	−3
Wigan	Chris Hutchings	−4
Wigan	Steve Bruce	0
Sunderland	Roy Keane	0
Middlesborough	Gareth Southgate	3
Reading	Steve Coppell	−1
Birmingham	Steve Bruce	−1
Birmingham	Alex McLeish	−1
Derby	Billy Davies	−1

2006/07 Championship	Manager	Difference
Sunderland	Roy Keane	0
Birmingham	Steve Bruce	0
WBA	Bryan Robson	0
WBA	Tony Mowbray	−1
Derby	Billy Davies	1
Southampton	George Burley	−1
Norwich	Nigel Worthington	−11

(Continued)

2006/07 Championship	Manager	Difference
Norwich	Peter Grant	−10
Wolves	Mick McCarthy	2
Leicester	Rob Kelly	−11
Ipswich	Jim Magilton	−5
Coventry	Micky Adams	−6
Coventry	Iain Dowie	−7
Cardiff	Dave Jones	−2
QPR	Gary Waddock	−17
QPR	John Gregory	−6
PNE	Paul Simpson	6
Burnley	Steve Cotterill	−1
Stoke	Tony Pulis	7
Hull	Phil Brown	−5
Sheff Wed	Paul Sturrock	0
Sheff Wed	Brian Laws	8
Plymouth	Ian Holloway	7

2006/07 Premier League	Manager	Difference
Chelsea	José Mourinho	−1
MU	Alex Ferguson	1
Arsenal	Arsène Wenger	−1
Liverpool	Rafael Benitez	1
Newcastle	Glenn Roeder	−8
West ham United	Alan Curbishley	−9

(Continued)

2006/07 Premier League	Manager	Difference
Tott	Martin Jol	2
AV	Martin O'Neill	−3
Everton	David Moyes	3
Middle	Gareth Southgate	−2
Portsmouth	Harry Redknapp	2
Blackburn	Mark Hughes	2
MC	Stuart Pearce	−1
Fulham	Chris Coleman	−1
Fulham	Lawrie Snachez	−2
Charlton	Alan Pardew	−4
Bolton	Sam Allardyce	9
Reading	Steve Coppell	9
Wigan	Paul Jewell	1
Sheffield United	Neil Warnock	1
Watford	Aidy Boothroyd	0

2005/06 Premier League	Manager	Difference
Chelsea	José Mourinho	0
MU	Alex Ferguson	0
Arsenal	Arsène Wenger	−1
Liverpool	Rafael Benitez	1
Newcastle	Graeme Souness	−2
Tott	Martin Jol	1
AV	David O'Leary	−9
Everton	David Moyes	−3

(*Continued*)

2005/06 Premier League	Manager	Difference
MC	Stuart Pearce	−6
Charlton	Alan Curbishley	−3
Blackburn	Mark Hughes	5
West ham United	Alan Pardew	3
Fulham	Chris Coleman	1
Bolton	Sam Allardyce	6
Birmingham City	Steve Bruce	−3
Portsmouth	Alain Perrin	1
Portsmouth	Harry Redknapp	−1
Wigan	Paul Jewell	7
WBA	Bryan Robson	0
Sunderland	Mick McCarthy	0

2005/06 Championship	Manager	Difference
Southampton	Harry Redknapp	−11
Southampton	George Burley	−11
Leeds United	Kevin Blackwell	−3
Norwich	Nigel Worthington	−6
Wolves	Glenn Hoddle	−3
Sheffield United	Neil Warnock	3
Reading	Steve Coppell	5
Leicester	Craig Levein	−9
Ipswich	Joe Royle	−7
Watford	Aidy Boothroyd	6

(Continued)

2005/06 Championship	Manager	Difference
Derby	Phil Brown	−10
Cardiff	Dave Jones	0
PNE	Billy Davies	8
Stoke	Johan Boskamp	0
Millwall	Colin Lee	−9
Millwall	David Tuttle	−9
Burnley	Steve Cotterill	−2
QPR	Ian Holloway	−5
Hull City	Peter Taylor	−1
Sheff Wed	Paul Sturrock	−1
Plymouth	Bobby Williamson	5
Plymouth	Tony Pulis	5
Brighton	Mark McGhee	−4
Crewe	Dario Gradi	−1

2004/05 Premier League	Manager	Difference
Chelsea	José Mourinho	0
MU	Alex Ferguson	−1
Arsenal	Arsène Wenger	1
Liverpool	Rafael Benitez	−1
Newcastle	Bobby Robson	−11
Newcastle	Graeme Souness	−9
MC	Kevin Keegan	−6
MC	Stuart Pearce	−2
Fulham	Chris Coleman	−6

2004/05 Premier League	Manager	Difference
Tott	Jacques Santini	−1
Tott	Martin Jol	−3
AV	David O'Leary	−1
Blackburn	Graeme Souness	−8
Blackburn	Mark Hughes	−5
Everton	David Moyes	7
Middles	Steve McClaren	5
Charlton	Alan Curbishley	2
Southampton	Harry Redknapp	−6
Birmingham City	Steve Bruce	−3
Bolton	Sam Allardyce	10
Portsmouth	Alain Perrin	1
WBA	Gary Megson	2
WBA	Bryan Robson	1
Norwich	Nigel Worthington	0

2004/05 Championship	Manager	Difference
West Ham	Alan Pardew	−5
Leeds	Kevin Blackwell	−13
Leicester	Micky Adams	−8
Leicester	Craig Levein	−12
Sunderland	Mick McCarthy	3
Wolves	Dave Jones	−4
Ipswich	Joe Royle	3
Reading	Steve Coppell	0

(Continued)

2004/05 Championship	Manager	Difference
Cardiff	Lennie Lawrence	−8
Derby	George Burley	5
Wigan	Paul Jewell	8
Nott For	Joe Kinnear	−12
Sheffield United	Neil Warnock	4
Millwall	Dennis Wise	3
Coventry	Micky Adams	−5
Watford	Ray Lewington	0
Watford	Aidy Boothroyd	−3
PNE	Craig Brown	2
PNE	Billy Davies	11
QPR	Ian Holloway	6
Stoke	Tony Pulis	6
Burnley	Steve Cotterill	6
Gillingham	Andy Hessenthaler	−1
Gillingham	Stan Ternent	−1
Brighton	Mark McGhee	1
Plymouth	Bobby Williamson	5
Crewe	Dario Gradi	1

2003/04 Prem League/ Championship	Manager	Difference
Chelsea	Claudio Ranieri	−1
MU	Alex Ferguson	−1
Arsenal	Arsène Wenger	2
Liverpool	Gerard Houllier	0

(*Continued*)

2003/04 Prem League/ Championship	Manager	Difference
Newcastle	Bobby Robson	0
MC	Kevin Keegan	−10
Leeds	Peter Reid	−13
Leeds	Eddie Gray	−12
Tott	Glenn Hoddle	−6
AV	David O'Leary	3
Everton	David Moyes	−7
Blackburn	Graeme Souness	−4
Fulham	Chris Coleman	3
Charlton	Alan Curbishley	6
Middles	Steve McClaren	7
Southampton	Gordon Strachan	5
Southampton	Paul Sturrock	4
Portsmouth	Harry Redknapp	3
Leicester	Micky Adams	−1
Bolton	Sam Allardyce	10
Birmingham	Steve Bruce	10
Portsmouth	Harry Redknapp	1
WBA	Gary Megson	3
Norwich	Nigel Worthington	3
West Ham	Alan Pardew	−3
Leeds	Peter Reid	−12
Sunderland	Mick McCarthy	−1
Wolves	Dave Jones	1

(Continued)

2003/04 Prem League/ Championship	Manager	Difference
Ipswich	Joe Royle	−2
Reading	Alan Pardew	6
Reading	Steve Coppell	−1
Cardiff	Lennie Lawrence	−6
Derby	George Burley	−18
Wigan	Paul Jewell	7
Nott For	Paul Hart	−4
Sheffield United	Neil Warnock	3
Millwall	Mark McGhee	6
Millwall	Dennis Wise	2
Coventry	Gary McAllister	0
Coventry	Eric Black	3
Coventry	Peter Reid	−3
Watford	Ray Lewington	−3
PNE	Craig Brown	0
QPR	Ian Holloway	6
Stoke	Tony Pulis	5
Burnley	Stan Ternent	−2
Gillingham	Andy Hessenthaler	−2
Brighton	Mark McGhee	1
Plymouth	Paul Sturrock	5
Crewe	Dario Gradi	3
Walsall	Colin Lee	−4
Rotherham	Ronnie Moore	2

Appendix 2 (as at 14/11/2008) Nationality of Premier League football managers from 2003–04 to 2007–08

	2003–04	2004–05	2005–06	2006–07	2007–08
English	Allardyce	Allardyce	Allardyce	Allardyce	Bruce
	Bobby Robson	McClaren	Pardew	Southgate	Coppell
	Curbishley	Keegan	Jewell	Pearce	Sanchez
	Bruce	Curbishley	Curbishley	Coppell	Curbishley
	McClaren	Bruce	McClaren	Redknapp	Redknapp
	Wigley (0.5)	Wigley (0.5)	Pearce	Jewell	Allardyce
	Redknapp (0.5)	Redknapp(0.5)	Redknapp	Pardew/Curbishley	Southgate
	Hoddle/Pleat	Bryan Robson	Bruce	Dowie/Reed/Pardew	Lee/Megson
	Keegan	Dowie	Bryan Robson	Warnock	
	Micky Adams		McCarthy	Boothroyd	
	Reid/Gray				
	Jones				

(Continued)

	2003–04	2004–05	2005–06	2006–07	2007–08
Other UK	Souness	Sturrock (0.5)	Ferguson	Ferguson	Ferguson
	Ferguson	Ferguson	Souness	Moyes	O'Neill
	Moyes	Hughes	Hughes	Hughes	Moyes
	Coleman	Moyes	Moyes	O'Neill	Davies
	Strachan (0.5)	Coleman	Coleman	Souness	Hughes
		Souness		Coleman	
		Worthington			
Non UK	Houllier	Perrin (0.5)	Mourinho	Mourinho	Keane
	Ranieri	Mourinho	Benitez	Benitez	Jol/Ramos
	O'Leary	Santini/Jol	Wenger	Wenger	Grant
	Wenger/Perrin (0.5)	Wenger	Jol	Jol	Wenger
		Benitez	O'Leary		Eriksson
		O'Leary			Benitez

Note: Where managers changed club and moved to a different grouping those are covered a half to each category.

Appendix 3 Teams in Premier League 1992–2009

Team	Seasons	Seasons in PL
Manchester United	1992 to date	17
Arsenal	1992 to date	17
Liverpool	1992 to date	17
Aston Villa	1992 to date	17
Norwich	1992–95, 2004–05	4
Blackburn	1992–99, 2001 to date	15
Newcastle	1993–2009	16
Middlesbrough	1992–93, 95–97, 98–09	14
Tottenham	1992 to date	17
Chelsea	1992 to date	17
Charlton	1998–99, 2000–07	8
Coventry	1992–2001	9
Manchester City	1992–96, 2000–01, 2002 to date	12
Crystal Palace	1992–3, 94–95, 97–98, 2004–05	4
Everton	1992 to date	17
QPR	1992–96	4
Sheffield Wednesday	1992–2000	8
Wimbledon	1992–2000	8
Sheffield United	1992–94, 2006–07	3
Ipswich Town	1992–95, 2000–02	5
Leicester	1994–95, 97–2002, 03–04	7
Leeds United	1992–2004	2

(Continued)

Team	Seasons	Seasons in PL
Southampton	1992–2005	3
Oldham Athletic	1992–94	2
Crystal Palace	1992–93, 94–98, 2004–05	6
Nottingham Forest	1992–93, 94–97, 98–99	5
Sunderland	1996–97, 99–2003, 05–06, 07 to date	8
Swindon	1993–94	1
West Ham United	1993–2003, 05 to date	14
Watford	1999–2000, 06–07	2
Bolton Wanderers	1995–96, 97–98, 2001 to date	10
Barnsley	1997–98	1
Derby	1996–2002, 07–08	7
WBA	2002–03, 04–06, 08–09	4
Bradford	1999–2001	2
Birmingham	2002–06, 07–08	5
Fulham	2001 to date	8
Wolverhampton	2003–04	1
Portsmouth	2003 to date	6
Wigan Athletic	2005 to date	4
Reading	2006–08	2
Hull	2008 to date	1
Stoke	2008 to date	1

Appendix 4 Football management progressions

Manager	From	To	Year
Tony Pulis	Bristol City	Portsmouth	2000
Tony Pulis	Plymouth	Stoke	2006
Steve Parkin	Rochdale	Barnsley	2001
Steve McClaren	Middlesbrough	England	2006
Steve Cotterill	Cheltenham	Stoke	2002
Steve Coppell	Brighton	Reading	2003
Steve Bruce	Crystal Palace	Birmingham	2001
Steve Bruce	Birmingham	Wigan	2007
Steve Bruce	Wigan	Sunderland	2009
Stan Ternent	Bury	Burnley	1998
Simon Grayson	Blackpool	Leeds	2008
Martin O'Neill	Wycombe	Norwich	1995
Martin O'Neill	Norwich	Leicester	1995
Martin O'Neill	Leicester	Celtic	2000
Brian Laws	Scunthorpe	Sheffield Wednesday	2006
Paul Ince	Macclesfield	MK Dons	2007
Paul Ince	MK Dons	Blackburn	2008
Paul Lambert	Colchester	Norwich	2009
Paul Simpson	Carlisle	Preston	2006
Paul Sturrock	Plymouth	Southampton	2004
Paul Sturrock	Swindon	Plymouth	2007
Mark Robins	Rotherham	Barnsley	2009
Peter Taylor	Gillingham	Leicester	2000
Phil Parkinson	Colchester	Hull	2006
Ray Harford	WBA	QPR	1997
Roberto Martinez	Swansea	Wigan	2009

(*Continued*)

Manager	From	To	Year
Sam Allardyce	Notts Co	Bolton	1999
Sam Allardyce	Bolton	Newcastle	2007
Sean O'Driscoll	Bournemouth	Doncaster	2006
Gordon Strachan	Southampton	Celtic	2004
George Burley	Southampton	Scotland	2008
Harry Redknapp	Portsmouth	Southampton	2004
Harry Redknapp	Southampton	Portsmouth	2005
Harry Redknapp	Portsmouth	Tottenham	2008
Howard Kendall	Sheffield United	Everton	1997
Iain Dowie	Oldham	Crystal Palace	2003
Ian Holloway	Plymouth	Leicester	2007
John Gregory	Wycombe Wanderers	Aston Villa	1998
John Gregory	Aston Villa	Derby	2002
John Ward	Cheltenham	Carlisle	2007
Kevin Keegan	Fulham	England	1999
Mark McGhee	Reading	Leicester	1994
Mark McGhee	Leicester	Wolverhampton	1995
Martin Allen	Brentford	MK Dons	2006
Martin Allen	MK Dons	Leicester	2007
Colin Calderwood	Northampton	Nottingham Forest	2006
Danny Wilson	Barnsley	Sheffield Wednesday	1998
Dave Jones	Stockport	Southampton	1997
David Moyes	Preston	Everton	2002
Dennis Wise	Swindon	Leeds	2006
Gary Johnson	Yeovil	Bristol City	2005
Gary Megson	Blackpool	Stockport	1997
Gary Megson	Leicester	Bolton	2007

(Continued)

Manager	From	To	Year
George Burley	Colchester	Ipswich	1994
George Graham	Leeds	Tottenham	1998
Gerry Francis	QPR	Tottenham	1994
Glenn Hoddle	Southampton	Tottenham	2001
Alan Pardew	Reading	West Ham	2003
Barry Fry	Southend	Birmingham	1993
Billy Davies	Preston	Derby	2006
Brian Horton	Oxford	Manchester City	1993
Brian Horton	Brighton	Port Vale	2004
Brian Little	Leicester	Aston Villa	1994
Brian Talbot	Rushden	Oldham	2004
Bruce Rioch	Bolton	Arsenal	1995
Chris Turner	Hartlepool	Sheffield Wednesday	2002

References

Allen, M. P., Panian, S. K. and Lotz, R. E. (1979) "Managerial succession and Organizational Performance: A Recalcitrant Problem Revisited", *Administrative Science Quarterly*, 21: 167–80.

Bain, A. (2005) "Constructing an Artistic Identity", *Work, Identity and Organisation*, 19, 1: 25–46.

Banning, K. (2004) "Corporate Governance and the New Chief Executive: How Institutionalized Power Affects the Agency Contract", *Corporate Ownership and Control*, 2, 1: Fall.

Berkeley Thomas, A. (1988) "Does Leadership Make a Difference to Organizational Performance?", *Administrative Science Quarterly*, 33: 388–400.

Bibeault, D. B. (1982) *Corporate Turnaround: How Managers Turn Losers into Winners* (New York: McGraw-Hill).

Birkbeck College (2006) *State of the Game Report*.

Blinde, E. M. and Greendorfer, S. L. (1985) "A Reconceptualisation of the Process of Leaving the Role of Professional Athlete", *International Review of Sport Sociology*, 20: 87– 94.

Boeker, W. (1992) "Power and Managerial Dismissal: Scapegoating at the Top", *Administrative Science Quarterly*, 37: 400–21.

Bolchover, D. and Brady, C. (2002) *The 90-Minute Manager: Business Lessons from the Dugout* (London: Prentice-Hall).

Bonazzi, G. (1983) "Scapegoating in Complex Organizations: The Results of a Comparative Study of Symbolic Blame-Giving in Italian and French Public Administration", *Organization Studies*, 4, 1: 1–18.

Bower, T. (2003) *Broken Dreams: The Vanity, Greed and the Souring of British Football* (London: Simon & Schuster).

Brewer, B. W. (1994) "Review and Critique of Models of Psychological Adjustment to Athletic Retirement", *Journal of Applied Sport Psychology*, 6, 11: 87–100.

Bridgewater, S., Kahn, L. and Goodall, A. (2010) "Substitution between Managers and Subordinates: Evidence from British Football", *IZA Discussion Papers*, 4589.

Brown, M. C. (1982) "Administrative Succession and Organizational Performance: The Succession Effect", *Administrative Science Quarterly*, 27: 1–16.

Bryman, A. (1986) *Leadership and Organization* (London: Routledge & Kegan Paul).

Bryman, A. (1989) "Leadership and Culture in Organizations", *Public Money and Management*, Autumn: 35–41.

Bryman, A. (1992) *Charisma and Leadership in Organizations* (Newbury Park, CA: Sage).

Burns, J. M. (1978) *Leadership,* (New York: Harper & Row).

Cyert, R. M. and March, J. G. (1963) *A Behavioural Theory of the Firm* (Engelwood Cliffs: Prentice-Hall).

Dai, C. F., Lewis, T. R. and Lopomo, G. (2006) "Delegating Management to Experts", *RAND Journal of Economics*, 37, 3: 503–20.

Dalton, D. R. and Kesner, I. F. (1985) "Organizational Performance as an Antecedent of Inside/Outside Chief Executive Succession: An Empirical Assessment", *Academy of Management Journal*, 28: 749–62.

Deloitte & Touche (2009) *Annual Review of Football Finance*.

Eitzen, D. S. and Yetzman, N. R. (1972) "Managerial Change, Longevity and Organizational Effectiveness", *Administrative Science Quarterly*, 17: 110–16.

Football Association (1991) *A Blueprint for English Football* (London: FA).

Fredrickson, J., Hambrick, D. C. and Baumrin, S. (1988) "A Model of CEO Dismissal", *Academy of Management Review*, 13: 255–70.

Fynn, A. and Guest, L. (1994) *Out of Time* (London: Simon & Shcuster).

Gamson, W. and Scotch, N. (1964) "Scapegoating in Baseball", *American Journal of Sociology,* 70: 69–76.

Gibson, L. D. (2005) "Blame Game", *Marketing Research,* Winter: 32–4.

Gilmore, S. (2000) "Football Management: Life in the Frying Pan", unpublished PhD thesis, University of Portsmouth.

Gilmore, S. and Gilson, C. (2007) "Finding Form: Elite Sports and the Business of Change", *Journal of Organizational Change Management,* 20, 3: 409–28.

Goodall, A. H. (2006) "Should Research Universities be Led by Top Researchers and Are They?", *Journal of Documentation*, 62, 3: 388–411.

Goodall, A. H. (2008) "Highly Cited Leaders and the Performance of Research Universities", Cornell Higher Education Research Institute, Working Paper Series, No. 111.

Goodall, A., Kahn, L. and Oswald, A. (2008) "Why Do Leaders Matter? The Role of Expert Knowledge", IZA Discussion Papers, 3583.

Green, C. (2002) *The Sack Race: The Story of Football's Gaffers* (Edinburgh and London: Mainstream Publishing).

Greiner, L. E. and Bhambri, A. (1989) "New CEO Intervention and Dynamics of Deliberate Strategic Change", *Strategic Management Journal*, 10: 67–87.

Grint, K. (2005) *The Sociology of Work* (Cambridge: Polity).

Grusky, O. (1960) "Administrative Succession in Formal Organizations", *Social Forces*, 39: 105–15.

Grusky, O. (1963) "Managerial Succession and Organizational Effectiveness", *American Journal of Sociology*, 69: 21–31.

Grusky, O. (1964) "Reply to Scapegoating in Baseball", *American Journal of Sociology*, 70: 72–76.

Hall, R. H. (1972) *Organizations, Structure and Process* (Englewood Cliffs: Prentice-Hall).

Hermalin, B. E. (1998) "Toward an Economic Theory of Leadership: Leading by Example", *American Economic Review*, 88, 5: 1188–206.

Hermalin, B. E. (2007) "Leading for the Long-term", *Journal of Economic Behaviour and Organization*, 62, 1: 1–19.

Hofer, C. W. (1980) "Turnaround Strategies", *Journal of Business Strategy*, 1: 19–31.

Hope, C. (2002) "When Should You Sack the Manager? Results from a Simple Model Applied to the English Premiership", Judge Institute of Management, Cambridge University, Research Paper No.2002/4.

House, R. (1971) "A Path-goal Theory of Leader Effectiveness", *Administrative Science Quarterly*, 16: 321–39.

Kahn, L. M. (1993) "Managerial Quality, Team Success and Individual Player Performance in Major League Baseball", *Industrial and Labor Relations Review*, 46, 3: 531–47.

Kerr, G. and Dacyshyn, A. (2000) "The Retirement Experience of Elite Female Gymnasts", *Journal of Applied Sport Psychology*, 12: 115–33.

Kesner, I. F. and Dalton, D. R. (1994) "Top Management Turnover and CEO Succession: An Investigation of the Effects of Turnover on Performance", *Journal of Management Studies*, 31, 5: September.

Kuper, S. and Szymanski, S. (2009) *Why England Lose: and Other Curious Phenomena Explained* (London: HarperCollins).

Leavy, B. and Wilson, D. C. (1994) *Strategy and Leadership* (London: Routledge).

Lieberson, S. and O'Connor, J. F. (1972) "Leadership and Organizational Performance: A Study of Large Corporations", *American Sociological Review*, 37: 117–30.

Mainiero, L. (1994) "Scapegoating Firm Performance: Which CEOs Get Away With It?", *Academy of Management Executive*, 8, 1: 77–78.

Majumdar, S. and Mukand, A. (2007) "The Leader as Catalyst: On Leadership and the Mechanics of Institutional Change", Working Paper 1128, Queens University, Canada.

McGillivray, D., Fearn, R. and McIntosh, A. (2005) "Caught Up in the Beautiful Game: A Case of Scottish Footballers", *Journal of Sport and Social Issues*, 29: 1: 102–23.

Moore, H. (1956) "Towards a Theory of Disaster", *American Sociological Review*, 21: 735.

Morley, I. E. (1984) "On Imagery and the Cycling of Decision-making", in J. G. Hunt, D. M. Hosking, C. A. Schriesheim and R. Stewart (eds), *Leaders and Managers: International Perspectives on Managerial Behavior and Leadership* (Oxford: NATO Scientific Affairs Symposium).

Nikolychuk, L. and Sturgess, B. (2007) "Managerial Performance and Contract Instability in the Market for National Football Coaches", *World Economics*, 8, 3: 147–70.

Peters, T. and Waterman, R. H. (1982) *In Search of Excellence: Lessons from America's Best-run Companies* (New York: Harper & Row).

Peters, T. and Austin, A. (1985) *A Passion for Excellence: The Leadership Difference* (New York: Random House).

Roderick, M. (2006) *The Work of Professional Football: A Labour of Love* (London and New York: Routledge).

Ronay, B. (2009) *The Absurd Ascent of the Most Important Man in Football* (London: Sphere).

Salancik, G. R. and Pfeffer, J. (1977) "Constraints on Administrator Discretion: The Limited Influence of Mayors on City Budgets", *Urban Affairs Quarterly*, 12: 475–98.

Samuelson, B. A., Galbraith, C. S. and McGuire, J. W. (1985) "Organizational Performance and Top-Management Turnover", *Organization Studies*, 1985: 6; 275.

Schendel, D. G., Patton, G. R. and Riggs, J. (1976) "Corporate Stagnation and Turnaround", *Journal of Economics and Business*, 28: 236–47.

Starbuck, W. H. and Hedberg, B. L. T. (1977) "Saving an Organization from a Stagnating Environment", in Thorelli, H. B. (ed.), *Strategy + Structure = Performance: The Strategic Imperative* (Bloomington: Indiana University Press): 249–58.

Stephan, Y. and Bilard, J. (2003) "Repercussions of Transition Out of Elite Sport on Body Image", *Perceptual and Motor Skills*, 96: 95–104.

Taylor Report (1989) The Hillsborough Stadium Disaster, The Home Office, 15 April, London.

Vroom, V. H. and Yetton, P. W. (1973) *Leadership and Decision-Making* (Pittsburgh: University of Pittsburgh Press).

Wacquant, L. J. D. (1995) "The Pugilistic Point of View: How Boxers Think and Feel About Their Trade", *Theory and Society*, 24, 4: 489–535.

Ward, A. (2003) *The Leadership Lifecycle: Matching Leaders to Evolving Organizations* (Basingstoke: Palgrave Macmillan).

Ward, A. and Williams, J. (2009) *Football Nation: Sixty Years of the Beautiful Game* (London: Bloomsbury).

Warriner, K. and Lavallee, D. (2008) "The Retirement Experiences of Elite Female Gymnasts: Self Identity and the Physical Self", *Journal of Applied Sport Psychology*, 20, 301–17.

Weiner, N. and Mahoney, T. A. (1981) "A Model of Corporate Performance as a Function of Environmental, Organizational and Leadership Influences", *Academy of Management Journal*, 24: 453–64.

Williams, J. (1996) "The New Football in England and Sir John Halls New Geordie Nation", in Gehrmann, S. (ed.), *Football and Regions in Europe* (Hamburg: LIT Verlag).

Williams, J. (1999) *Behind the Headlines: Is It All Over? Can Football Survive the Premier League?* (Reading, UK: South Street Press).

Index